About the author

David Cohen was born and raised in Manchester, but he hopes you won't hold that against him. His career in dental practice spans almost fifty years, most recently specialising in endodontics, but along the way he has been a postman, an unofficial tour guide and a chauffeur. Officially, his professional title is Dr Dr Cohen. He has been married to Marsha, the lady he once introduced as "my first wife," for fifty-two years and they have three children and six grandchildren, all of whom, one way or another, have made their own contributions to the book.

The author says he can't see himself retiring any time soon — from anything.

This is a work of non-fiction. All of the anecdotes contained in these pages are true but they have been 'humourised' for effect. Some names have been changed, some have been made up due to lack of correct memory, and some are actual. Nothing in this book is intended to cause offence or insult.

A Mouthful of Humour
the dentist bites back

Dr B David Cohen

A Mouthful of Humour
the dentist bites back

Vanguard Press

VANGUARD PAPERBACK

© Copyright 2023
Dr B David Cohen

The right of Dr B David Cohen to be identified as author of
this work has been asserted by him in accordance with the
Copyright, Designs and Patents Act 1988.

All Rights Reserved

No reproduction, copy or transmission of this publication
may be made without written permission.
No paragraph of this publication may be reproduced,
copied or transmitted save with the written permission of the
publisher, or in accordance with the provisions
of the Copyright Act 1956 (as amended).

Any person who commits any unauthorised act in relation to
this publication may be liable to criminal
prosecution and civil claims for damages.

A CIP catalogue record for this title is
available from the British Library.

ISBN 978-1-80016-565-6

Vanguard Press is an imprint of
Pegasus Elliot Mackenzie Publishers Ltd.
www.pegasuspublishers.com

First Published in 2023

Vanguard Press
Sheraton House Castle Park
Cambridge England

Printed & Bound in Great Britain

Dedication

This book is dedicated to my parents, Debbie and Phil, who helped and supported me in my goal of realising a career in dentistry, and to my wife, Marsha, who has put up with me for over fifty years, once I had achieved that goal.

Acknowledgements

It goes without saying, but I'll say it anyway, that I am grateful to all of those people who have featured — be that wittingly or otherwise — in the various stories recounted in these pages. Of course I am, because without them, the pages would be blank.

Being a man who wishes to continue to be fed and watered, I would like to show my appreciation for Marsha, my long-suffering wife of over fifty-two years (that's right, we were *very* young when we married, mere whippersnappers) who, although having accepted me for better or worse, couldn't have known at the time that this would involve writing a book.

I thank my family: sons, Gary and Johnny; daughter, Lisa; daughters-in-law, Caroline and Lauren; son-in-law, Salman, and six adorable, fabulous grandchildren, Josh, Ellie, Libby, Marissa, Sammy and Freddie, all of whom either feature or have contributed in some way to this tome. Please note that no small children were harmed in the production, although some may have been bribed.

To my professional colleagues, past and present, business partners and bosses, nurses and receptionists, and everyone who has been a part of my meteoric rise to being able to wear a white coat (for some reason now called 'scrubs' and not even white nowadays) and poke about in people's gobs, I say *thank you,* and maybe one day you will be able to find it in your heart to forgive me for my portrayal of your good selves. Dare I say, you might even buy a copy, which I will gladly sign if requested, and with the appropriate fee paid (only joking).

Finally, a word of thanks to my writer, Maggie Allen (www.the-write-word.co.uk), for telling me off, putting me right when I was clearly disappointingly wrong, for refusing point-blank to include some stories that I thought should be included, because "that's just not funny, David, not in a month of Sundays", and basically for turning my original (not professional) writing into professional writing, or what she calls 'bookspeak'. My thanks also to The Ghostwriting Company (www.ghostwritingcompany.co.uk) for introducing us.

Introduction

Having given almost fifty years to my career in dentistry, and before that, having trained and qualified to do so (because they like us to be qualified), I can honestly say I never once saw myself as an author of anything except professional documents, theses and so on. And certainly not as a writer. Good writing is something I appreciate and admire, and sometimes even understand, but I would never consider dipping my toe in that water — or, perhaps, inkwell.

What happened was, over the years I had become a collector of various things — quite an eclectic mix of items with no particular theme, and at some point, I realised one of these was a pretty sizeable gathering of little stories, featuring different topics, times, places and people. I would find myself dropping some of these anecdotes into my lectures and talks (only where professionally applicable, of course) and at other times I'd just be reminded of an incident from the past so I'd tell whichever tale to whoever wanted to listen, or perhaps those who had no visible means of escape.

The more I realised this was another 'collection', the more I wondered how best to compile it, to structure it, to give it *an identity*. I also didn't want to lose any of my little tales of yore (well, some of them go as far back as yore), to allow them to fall victim to the passage of time and be lost forever. Some people, presumably those who really enjoyed my tale-telling, would say, *My goodness! You should write a book — I'd buy it!*

That led to discussion, mainly with family and friends, including a cousin who is a real live journalist, and she encouraged my quest — not that I (or my quest) needed any encouragement, once I'd caught the Book Bug.

But how to get from me having all of these little stories, to producing a book? The Unknown Territory. In short, I found an agency, and they found me a writer, and off we went. It's been a very different experience from anything I've done before, but at last my collection of words and memories has an identity — ladies and gentlemen, allow me to introduce *A Mouthful of Humour — The Dentist Bites Back*.

Out of the mouth of babes...[¥]

My Grandpa David is great. He's Max's half-grandpa as well. Max is my first cousin and his grandpa lives in Liverpool so I let him adopt my Grandpa David.

We talk most mornings on FaceTime on the way to school. It's me going to school, not Grandpa. He always calls me Captain Obvious and asks me, *How you doodling?*

I always remember going to his surgery to check my teeth, and leaving with a bag of chocs. Then Mum and I got lost on the way home.

A few years ago, when Mummy and Daddy went on holiday, Grandpa had just had a back operation. I helped him get better by walking with him every day. He was very slow, even slower than me and I was only small.

I also love going to Grandma and Grandpa's house at the weekend. We play bingo and snakes and ladders. Grandma said tell them we never play for money. We

---

[¥] A quotation from the King James Bible, Psalms 8:2, a psalm of David, and with apologies to David and King James, technically, it should read 'Out of the mouths of babes' but who am I to argue with a King?

play table tennis as well but the problem is that he beats me.

Freddie, aged 8

***

My Grandpa is one of the most adventurous people I know. But he's definitely not the sportiest.

I will never forget, a few years ago in Spain he agreed to play football, I think for the first time in his adult life, and within a few minutes he tripped over the ball and broke his ankle. Next thing, a massive ambulance turned up and took him to hospital. It was funny because Grandma was too small to climb into the ambulance and had to be lifted up. The good thing is that, on the way home, we jumped all the queues at the airport. That was cool.

Grandpa really enjoys his toys, not like most other grandpas I know. My Daddy took me to see Grandpa's plane once, but Mummy wouldn't let me go up in it, even when I told her it was all right because Grandpa passed his test.

I am so pleased Grandpa is a dentist. When someone at school threw a tennis ball at my mouth by accident, it hurt a lot but Grandpa made it okay. Once, Mummy took me and my brother to his surgery and he checked all our teeth. Then he gave us chocolate. Best dentist ever!

Since lockdown, we don't visit Grandma and Grandpa but he organises a big Zoom call with all the family on a Friday at half past six, which is great. But we can't play table tennis on Zoom.

Sammy, aged 11

***

My Grandpa is very kind and very funny, and he loves doing adventurous things.

One of my favourite memories is when we used to get comfy on the couch and watch our special programme on TV, *Chockywockydoodah*. We both loved it because it was all about our very favourite thing, chocolate. That isn't one of the adventurous things, just so you know.

Grandpa even took me to the *Chockywockydoodah* shop, all the way in London. He always brought us chocolate from everywhere he went, even when we weren't allowed. He spoiled us with bags and bags of it because he knew we loved it so much. Maybe I should leave the bit out about us not being allowed chocolate.

Even when Grandpa checked mine and my brother's teeth to make sure they were all okay, he made going to the dentist good fun! There are not many dentists who you visit and come out with a bag of chocolates.

I love spending time with Grandpa and one of my favourites is our weekly Zoom calls on Friday. As we couldn't see much of each other in real life for the past year or so, he made sure we still had a big family catch-up and it was really special to everybody.

With his boat, plane, motorbikes and cars, Grandpa is one of the coolest! I love listening to his stories and seeing videos of him flying his plane. I was only little at the time but I enjoy the pictures of when he used to take us out on the boat in Spain. It's funny looking at pictures of yourself when you were young and you can't remember.

Now you know all my favourite things about Grandpa, especially the chocolate.

Marissa, aged 14

***

I feel very lucky to have a grandpa like Grandpa David. Because of how far apart we live, we can only speak on the phone normally but we have our weekly FaceTime catch-ups as well.

Luckily, I have had no experience of Grandpa as a dentist, not like the rest of the family. I mean it's lucky I didn't need anything doing to my teeth, not that I wouldn't want Grandpa to do it. Writing can be tricky sometimes.

We all admire Grandpa for his adventurous side, with his motorbikes and flying his plane. He would sometimes come down to visit in the plane, which was really cool! We didn't have a massive garden so he landed at the local airfield.

My personal favourite has to be the boat and I would look forward to our holidays in Spain and taking the boat out on the sea. Sometimes Grandpa let me drive! Now I'm older, I wonder if maybe I wasn't really driving it, but it was great fun anyway.

Once Grandpa and Grandma took Libby and I to Florence and it was amazing just spending time with them, even when we had to keep stopping so Grandpa could have another coffee. I don't know why he needs so much coffee.

I'm proud of Grandpa's efforts in writing this book, and it's good that he found someone to help him a bit.

Ellie, aged 16

***

One of my earliest memories of Grandpa is when we were all on holiday in Spain and I had a wobbly tooth.

I was way too scared to pull it out in any way that would hurt, and that was definitely all of them. Well, that's what I thought until Grandpa David came to the rescue. Once I'd stopped crying hysterically, he sat me down and did something to distract me, then — without me feeling a thing — my loose tooth was out! How cool was that.

It's not just Grandpa's dentist skills that make him the coolest grandpa; there is much more, like having a real pilot's licence! That means the licence is real, not the pilot, even though Grandpa is real as well. And he had his own real plane.

I do remember Grandpa's boat and always looked forward to summer holidays so we could go out for a day trip or just a quick ride along the coast. Grandpa would let me drive the boat myself and that's a really cool memory. I know I never flew the plane, because I was only very young.

Grandpa gives really good advice, and recently he told me that I should "always think one step ahead" and I know that will help me in any situation. When I'm with Grandpa David sometimes it's easy to think ahead because I know for certain he will need to stop for another coffee soon.

Libby, aged 16

***

When I was younger, I used to see my Grandpa as a real live Action Man as well as a dentist, and I would tell all my friends how cool he was.

Not only could he pull my wobbly teeth out, and anyone else's for that matter, but he had a pilot's licence, and his own plane! I told my mates how he taught me to drive the plane.

The third thing, and my favourite, was that he drove his own boat. It was always the highlight of my summer to go on the boat and Grandpa letting me drive that.

You really couldn't get much cooler as a grandpa, and he would always give me his best advice when it came to the important things such as work, and fighting with my parents. I suppose all teenagers do that (the fighting, not the work).

Now I'm older, it's as if our roles have kind of reversed, an example being when Grandpa asked me what I thought of the car he was about to buy, and I told him it was too feminine for him. I think he took what I said to heart because he cancelled the order and chose a different car, one I approved of!

Something we all comment on is Grandpa's inability to go more than five minutes, wherever we are, without having to get another coffee. He always says it's Grandma who needs to stop, but we know the truth!

Anyway, my Grandpa is the best I could wish for, always there for me if I need his help or advice (or sometimes cash!) and I can't wait for more cars, holidays — and, of course, cups of coffee!

Joshua, aged 20

Murder or Mystery...

You've killed her! Everyone in the room was screaming.

Except me. I was the one they were screaming at.

No, I haven't! I screamed back, hoping I was clinging on to some tiny scrap of professionalism, although my high-pitched girly shriek had probably put paid to that.

It was Christmas Day, sometime in the early 1970s, and Slade were singing *Merry Christmas, Everybody* (again). Me — I was in a stranger's home, surrounded by some very angry people, also strangers, being accused of murder. And, quite possibly, in danger of being lynched.

I gulped, and stared at the young woman lying on the couch in front of me — completely motionless.

What had led to me being the centre of this rather undesirable attention in a not-very-festive, but nonetheless very real, drama, was nothing more than my attempt to build my new dental practice business, by taking out-of-hours emergency calls, very often at the patient's home.

The distraught female on the other end of the phone line had obviously been in agony with toothache, which she'd been suffering from for several days and which was preventing her from getting any sleep. Even the sleeping tablets she'd taken weren't working because the pain was so severe. How could I refuse? A damsel in dental distress and the opportunity to earn my magnificent call-out fee of ten pounds. So off I'd trotted.

Once I'd checked out the situation and decided the only solution was to extract the offending tooth, I administered an injection of local anaesthetic and waited while it took effect.

The effect was not quite what I expected. It appears that, as soon as the affected area became numb, hence the pain instantly disappeared, the sleeping tablets just kicked in and my patient... well, she sort of... collapsed. Her eyelids clamped shut, her head lolled to one side and she slumped, like a drunken rag doll, in a seemingly comatose heap on the couch.

That's when her relatives started screaming at me, and I suppose I can't really blame them. She didn't look altogether very... well, *alive*. She may have been the one in the deep sleep, but I was definitely the one living the nightmare.

I managed to pull myself together enough to check the lady's vital signs, if for no other reason than to prevent the massive coronary heading my way, and to convince the relatives, who, at this point, were not incredibly receptive to being convinced of anything, especially not by Yours Truly, anyway, that she was fine, just sleeping because of the medication she'd been taking. The next thing I managed was to wake her up.

It was possibly the speediest extraction of my career to date, removing the tooth and then removing myself, equally speedily, from the scene, not forgetting to grab my ten-pound fee as I went!

Getting there... wherever 'there' is

Hello, reader, whoever and wherever you are.

With regard to the *whoever,* as you are actually reading this, I reckon it's a fairly safe bet that you are in one of two categories. One, my family (each member of which fine institution will, no doubt, be expecting a free copy) or two, a patient from the past, in which case you are probably already drafting instructions to your solicitor to sue me, either because I mention you and your dental problems in the forthcoming pages, or because I omit to mention you. Damned if I do, etc.

With this Sword of Damocles hanging precariously over me, but in its twenty-first-century guise as General Data Protection Regulation, I won't be talking out of school about anybody — or maybe I'll just change the names to protect the innocent.

And, as to the *wherever,* given today's technology bombarding every area of our lives, plus a few more besides, you could be anywhere in the universe (well, as long as it's an 'anywhere' with a breathable atmosphere) with your Kindle tucked into your thong, mankini or hermetically sealed Eskimo suit. I mention this with absolutely no connection to, or sponsorship from, Amazon. Come to think of it, you could actually be *on* the Amazon!

This book, thesis, essay, or whatever you like to call it, is neither a diary (which seems to be the 'in' thing these days) because I never kept one (which, incidentally, I suspect some of those who won fame and fortune as diarists, didn't, either) nor is it an autobiography, basically because I'm nowhere near interesting enough.

As I set out on this mission, I must confess to a couple of things. Firstly, and in my own opinion, I am a very poor writer. The only previous writing, allegedly of some substance, I have ever completed was in the form of my two theses, PhD and MSc, although I imagine their success was more to do with the information contained within them, rather than the way the words were put together.

I am certainly not as good a writer as my journalist cousin, or — to be more scientifically accurate, which I feel my qualifications in biomaterials science entitle me to state — my cousin-in-law. So, I have written this volume in its original form, and then my writer (yes, a real writer) has worked her magic on it, so let's call it a joint effort, shall we?

So, as the Great Writer once said, *I am writing this very slowly, as I know you cannot read very fast.* Only joking, and anyway, I'm not writing — I'm typing. And that, in my case, is very slowly indeed.

Secondly, I have a severe needle phobia, so you'll agree that dentistry probably wouldn't necessarily be my first career choice. However, I soon discovered that needles have two ends, and they are very different — the sharp end, and the good end. I prefer to stay at the good end, to be blunt about it.

The times in my life when I have to be on the sharp end have always proved an excellent opportunity for me to shed a few pounds, because I am so fearful and perspire so much before and throughout the procedure, that I actually lose weight.

Many years ago, I fainted, totally out of it, after having a jab in preparation for travelling abroad. I'd managed to find a discreet little clinic where I thought I'd be able to keep my embarrassing condition hush-hush, and nobody I knew would have to discover my extreme reaction to the needle. But when I arrived, I discovered to my horror that the doctor about to give me the shot was a friend of mine. Luckily for me, he remained totally professional and never mentioned it to me, nor anyone else… as far as I know!

So, why did I choose dentistry as a career?

Please note at this point, I am not what is referred to in the trade as a frustrated medic, someone who couldn't get into medical school so tried dentistry instead.

It all began when I was seven and was attending the long-established dental practice of one, David Blain. No, not that David Blaine, the illusionist — although this one reckoned he could make tooth decay disappear with the aid of a drill, if not a top hat and a rabbit.

On the subject of drills, David — yes, I can call him by his first name now, because (a) we eventually became colleagues and he would refer patients to me for specialist treatment, but mainly (b) because he is dead. Anyway, David was one of the first dentists in the UK to have the high-speed drill, or turbine, as it was known. The reason for this is another little story…

After graduating from Manchester University, David was persuaded — possibly by his surgeon uncle and also by his lecturer at the dental school, Dr Holt, who had himself done the same years before — to travel all the way to Chicago to gain a US dental degree. And so, off he went with his young wife, Rosalyn, in tow. In due course, he graduated as an American dentist and then they returned to the UK.

I believe that, while at dental school in Chicago, David must have had access to this latest innovation, the high-speed drill (as opposed to the not-so-high-speed drill), and brought it back with him to the UK when he came home and opened up in practice.

David and Rosalyn had a very large house in Manchester and so, quite sensibly, he opened his dental practice in two of their front rooms, providing a surgery and a waiting room.

On the wall in the waiting room hung a framed photograph — one of those elongated black-and-white school photos that every educational institution had taken, the production of which was always a nightmare, with much tie-straightening, gravy-stain-removing, fringe-combing and attempting to get a whole school full of pupils to both stand still *and* try to appear at least semi-human. The procedure always seemed to take an eternity, while the photographer slowly panned the camera from one end of the rows of pupils (mainly grimacing) and teachers (mainly sour-faced) to the other.

This clever photographic technique (oh, yes, it really was, back in the day) opened up the possibility for the school clown (every school had one) to stand to attention at the extreme end of one row where the photographer was beginning the shoot, duck behind the back row of pupils and make his way to the other end, where he would take up his position at the end of the same row. So, when the photo was developed and printed, the same boy (it was always a boy, no idea why) could clearly be seen in the two opposite places. And he was always grinning.

Anyway, this photo in David's waiting room was of his graduation year at the Northwestern University Dental School in Chicago. Every time I had an appointment with him, I would spend my whole time in that room scanning the photo from side to side, up and down the rows of happy faces, and I never, ever, found David in the picture. That's a lot of searching to come up with no result. It became something of a minor obsession, every time I went, right up to when it was my turn to go to dental school. Mystery.

I never forgot that photo and years later, when I heard that David had died, I wrote a letter of condolence to Rosalyn and their daughter, Susan. While writing, I mentioned that I would be most grateful to receive a copy of the photo, for old times' sake. Rosalyn graciously agreed to send me one when she and Susan had sorted David's affairs.

So, back to my explanation as to my career choice: I do believe it was due to my admiration for David Blain and his achievements, not to mention the mystery of his non-appearance in that school photo, which still fascinates me to this day.

Haggis and Tunny Fish

Just popping back into the annals of history, back to my salad days, my time at grammar school…

I think every school had *that teacher,* the one who stood out as a particularly nasty piece of work, the one who had obviously trained under a resurrected Vlad the Impaler, and who would probably be cocky enough to start an argument with Idi Amin.

For me, this was a chap we'd nicknamed Haggis (I'm guessing we did that because he was Scottish and because schoolboy humour is very basic) who taught geography and PE. For some reason never to be revealed to me, he took a dislike to Yours Truly around the time I started wearing a signet ring.

The ring was a gift from some friends of my parents to mark my *bar mitzvah*, when, at the ripe old age of thirteen, I was declared to be a man, as per the ages-old Jewish tradition. Maybe the idea is that you are given gifts that you can hold close to you because you have just been divested of something that *was* very close to you.

Anyway, Haggis wasn't happy with this ring-wearing Jewish kid, so he took it upon himself to confiscate it. *He* took *my* ring and wouldn't give it back.

I wasn't impressed, and where was Mr Amin when I needed him? Adding insult to injury, Haggis made me write a four-page essay. Not an essay on Jewish traditions, or gift giving, and definitely not on jewellery for men. An essay on tunny fish, my punishment for wearing my own ring.

Now, don't misunderstand me, I do believe in people being punished *if they have committed a wrongdoing.* But I firmly believed there had been no doing of wrong, and in what universe can it be seen as wrong to wear a ring that was a symbol of a massive milestone in my life, my passage into manhood? No wonder kids grow up confused about what's right and what's wrong.

Back to the tunny fish. What an obscure topic, of all the things he could have come up with. Tunny fish. Not *tuna,* that would have been too easy, because I could have written about the tin of tuna in the kitchen cupboard at home, about the tuna pasta my mother made, about the nutritional benefits of said fish as described on the label of the tin. Yes, I could have filled four pages easily.

But no, I had to find out about tunny fish. Finding out about anything was, in those days, something that took a lot of time and effort, seeing as there was no internet, no websites, no computers and no mobile phones. Any and all such research had to be done by ploughing through reference books and encyclopaedias — there's a blast from the past!

Haggis also knew how to play the mind games, the psychological angle, as well as dishing out cruel penalties for things that really didn't warrant any penalty at all. Every time I did something good (in his opinion, so it didn't happen often) he would reduce the essay task by one page.

Equally, whenever I did something bad (in his opinion, so it happened a lot) he would increase the number of pages again. As you can imagine, this tunny fish essay became something of a tome.

Luckily for me, my mother took pity on her ringless, fish-facts-seeking child and helped me write the totally pointless essay. I have to say, I'd have been a lot happier if her level of pity had been sufficient to move her into putting in an official complaint to the school about Haggis' treatment of her offspring, but, sadly, 'twas not to be.

Eventually, pages written, the world of the lowly tunny fish fully explored and essay submitted, my precious ring (no not *that* precious ring as per Mr Tolkien) (you can look up Tolkien if you like) was duly returned to its rightful owner.

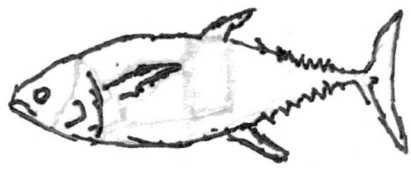

Tunny Fish by Freddie, aged 8

Going Back to School

To reach the dizzy heights of becoming a fully-fledged dentist in the UK — and I'm specifying that purposely since I can't comment on this aspect for any other country, territory, state, planet or universe — you need to attend dental school. This usually happens straight after secondary school, which, in my own case, was the late, but probably not lamented, Stand Grammar School for Boys.

By the way, Stand Grammar School for Boys has been demolished and replaced with a housing estate. In fact, my son actually bought a house on this estate, which stood on the same piece of land (give or take a couple of yards) as Room 5, my very first form classroom in 1959 when I took my very first plimsoll-clad steps as a pupil there. Later, my daughter bought a flat on the estate, which was built, apparently, where the playing field had been, although, as my attachment to sport has always been tenuous at best, I have to take her word for that. For information, I do have a number of rules that I live by, and number one is SK *(Sport Kills)*.

I don't know how it is now, but back in those long-lost days when I was applying for dental school, we were allowed to apply to four or five schools through the UCCA system, and, as well as that generous spread of potential opportunities, we could also apply to all London-based schools, of which I seem to remember there were five, because they had not yet signed up to the UCCA[¥] system.

I applied to as many schools as was physically possible, of course, not wishing to leave it too much to chance (or any other Monopoly board location), and each application met with one of these four responses:

Outright rejection — from those who will never know what they missed

Offer of interview — from those who can spot quality

A conditional offer — they spotted it, too, but with more confidence

Being put on a waiting list — me waiting for them to see sense?

Shock, horror! My ego was almost knocked unconscious from the blows raining down on the poor thing, in the form of rejection letters. My dejection at the rejection, however, was cured by two offers of interview, from King's College and the Royal Dental Hospital, both in London, and which were received within two days of each other.

Oddly, a close pal from grammar school was also applying for dental school and had been offered

---

[¥] UCCA: Universities Central Council on Admissions, providing a clearing house for university applications in the UK from 1961 to 1993 interviews at the same two places — and on the same days! I did wonder if these establishments only bothered to do one letter and sent the same to everybody, and was intrigued to see how many of us would all turn up at the same time.

So, the two of us trundled off to the Big City, on the train, which was a novelty in those days. While I stayed at the Regent Palace Hotel, in my young and inexperienced eyes a magnificent establishment, my friend stayed with family.

To get to Denmark Hill for our King's College interviews, we took the tube, which was a serious novelty, even more so than the train journey, then a bus ride, which wasn't any kind of novelty, seeing as we had buses up north.

As we were getting off said bus, this man in front of us suddenly collapsed and fell to the floor, flailing about all over the place — and we had not the slightest, foggiest clue what to do. Then this other chap came forward, and it turned out he was a consultant pathologist (what are the chances? No, really, what are they?).

He very calmly diagnosed an epileptic fit and dealt with the poor flailing chap, thank heaven, because we (the definitely *not* calm people) couldn't have done anything. To this day, I remember what the pathologist said to us.

Sorry, boys, I'm not used to this — I usually see them after they've died.

He thought that was funny. We really didn't.

Anyway, having arrived at King's, we were each sat at a desk on which had been placed a block of wax about three inches square (actually, to be scientifically correct, it was *cubed*), a long piece of wire, a sheet of paper on which was printed a drawing of a coat hanger shape, a pair of wire-bending pliers (we later learned that these were orthodontic pliers), and a large knife (more later learning, this time of a 'wax knife', also regularly used in dentistry).

We were then asked — no, that's not quite true, we were *told*, and in no uncertain terms — to carve a pyramid from the wax block, and bend the wire into the coat hanger shape as on the paper.

It soon became apparent that the interviewers had conducted this weird exercise on at least one previous occasion, by the appearance of a large box of sticking plasters, which came in very useful when most of us managed to stick either the wire or the knife into our fingers and/or hands at some point. I gave it my best shot, piercing myself in the attempt, thus requiring the services of the box of plasters.

It transpired that the reason for this strange — not to mention, dangerous — test was that King's College Dental School, London (having already caused me personal injury, I now respectfully use its official full title) was researching the comparison between manual dexterity at interview stage and the same at graduation. This could only be examined if you were accepted on the course, of course. Not me, as it turned out. I wonder if they needed the plasters quite as much at the graduation end of the exercise.

When I did get to dental school (not King's, as I said) a chap in my year eventually ended up as Head of Restorative Dentistry at King's and he was able to access the results of this investigation into dexterity. Guess what? Yes, you guessed — absolutely no correlation whatsoever, so all of our stab wounds and lifetime scars were for nothing.

As the outcome of this test and the interview was that I received a rejection letter to add to my collection, I never had the chance to take part in the unsuccessful dexterity research programme. I bet the whole thing cost someone a lot of money. And all wasted! But, hey! Never mind, someone probably got an MSc or even a PhD, so not *all* in vain.

Anyway, back to the interviews. Next day, my friend and I (let's call him Phil, shall we? That was his name, after all, and still is) trotted off to The Royal Dental Hospital of London, in the very up-market (in those days it was) Leicester Square.

Our interviews were conducted by a rather stern Dean, Professor Raleigh Barclay Lucas (just Googled him and yes, that was his name, and in the correct sequence). Incidentally, that search revealed that he wasn't even a dentist, he was an oral pathologist, and he asked what appeared to be extremely irrelevant questions. Well, he would, wouldn't he? Seeing as he wasn't a dentist.

After the interviews, Phil and I decided to really hit the big time for lunch and so, as one does (or even both of us) when one is in Leicester Square, we went into the Golden Egg — which was conveniently located on the ground floor of the Dental Hospital. The place was teeming with excited kids who had all just had their interviews with Prof. Raleigh Barclay Lucas. One of the young ladies we got talking to — we were hitting the big time, remember, so we had to chat up at least one female — was Mary (that really was her real name) who was also hoping to get a place at The Royal.

Coincidentally, (if you believe in coincidence) when I did eventually get a place at The Royal, one of the first people I bumped into was — of course — Mary.

To avoid further long versions of short stories, I wasn't even offered a reserve place at The Royal Dental Hospital of London.

Some months later, I sat my A-levels in Physics, Chemistry and Zoology (yes, really, the person who isn't at all fond of any animals took Zoology). Needless to say, I didn't excel in some subjects, and managed to obtain (you really think I would reveal my grades?) some rather disappointing results.

Dad, Mum and I were all gutted to receive this news, but Mum, whose glass was always half full (usually with whisky), told me and Dad to *Get down to Dad's office and don't you come home 'til you've phoned all the dental schools and got a place to do dentistry!*

So, off we toddled, rooted out all the phone numbers and began ringing them, every single one, driven perhaps not so much by the need for me to find a place, but for the pair of us to be fed some dinner before nightfall.

Back then, long-distance phone calls (in this case, anywhere outside Manchester) were quite expensive and this little exercise must have cost Dad, or maybe his business, a small fortune. But it was worth it, Dad — really. Or, should I say, *I was worth it!*

When we got through to the Admissions Secretary at the Royal Dental Hospital, Leicester Square, London, a lady whose name was Beryl D. Cottell, thereby giving her initials that she shared with my good self, we had the strangest response...

Well, actually, we've got one place left and you might as well have it.

And — exhale!

***

Looking back at those interviews today, given how things have changed (and not necessarily for the better, I assure you), they should have focused more on manual dexterity, but in the form of a typing test.

Today's dentists spend so much time keeping records, logging information into a computer and so on, they might have been well advised to check our keyboard skills. So, you want to be a dentist, do you? Can you type? No? Sorry — you need to choose a different profession.

***

As a result of the consolidation of dental schools in London, after I left The Royal in 1971 it was amalgamated with (i.e., taken over by) Guy's Dental Hospital, which itself was eventually amalgamated with St Thomas's *and* King's! So, now, despite everything that transpired in 1966, I am officially an alumnus (someone who graduated there) of King's, and to think, I only ever visited that place once for the interview (not forgetting the self-imposed injuries, too).

As I write this, I have just opened a mailshot from 'Guy's, King's and St Thomas's', asking for financial support. I guess it's to keep them in plasters, just in case! I wonder if they would accept a donation of Elastoplast?

Finding Digs

Was ever a man so grateful to a woman who was neither his wife nor his mother? I wonder. But I was (and have remained, because I'm nothing if not constant) exceedingly grateful to Beryl D. Cottell for securing my place at dental school.

As I was the very first member of my family ever to attend university, the experience was all completely new to us, and all the more exciting because I, a true northerner, was also heading off to The Big Smoke (I was hoping some of it might have cleared by the time I arrived), leaving home for the first time to live in the capital city. London, in all its overcrowded, bustling, glitzy glory. There was much to be done.

I'm surprised our letterbox didn't break, with the amount and frequency of correspondence that kept arriving from the dental school — you have to remember there was no email in those days, no internet, no tweeting, nor any of those other twenty-first-century technological oddities that seem hell bent on turning everyone into a hermit, glued to a computer screen and keyboard. So, if you needed something to be *in writing* it had to be sent as a letter.

We had letters. Oh, we had letters! There was a letter telling me what items I should take with me, another letter telling me which books I should buy, another letter telling me which surgical instruments I needed to buy... so many letters.

This resulted in many excursions to various shops and supply companies of the relevant items. I repeat, I said there was *no internet,* therefore there was *no internet shopping,* however difficult you may find that concept.

For example, because we (students, not my family) would be carrying out some dissection work, a dissection kit was required, and this is *not* something you would have found in the local Woolworth store, even when they were open. The instruments (one of every single item we could ever possibly need) were supplied in a solid wooden box that seemed to weigh about half a ton on a good day, and it had to be lugged around the dental school, once we got there.

One of the letters very helpfully provided me with a list of dental supply companies and one of these companies had a branch in Manchester, so off Dad and I trotted to the premises of Messrs S. S. White to purchase the requisite instruments. Of course, neither of us had the foggiest idea what we were buying, but the list that came through the letterbox had been very specific and informative, and also these companies were extremely professional, avoiding Dad and Yours Truly ending up with a collection of useless scrap metal.

When it came to the lab coat I needed (to at least give the illusion that we students knew something about something vaguely medical), my grandmother had been involved in — would you Adam and Eve it? (just practising for the London lifestyle) — the lab coat manufacturing industry, so I was able to grab as many white coats as I desired, from the family business. Thanks, Gran!

Then there was the question of somewhere for me to live. I had no interest in taking student accommodation, even if such had been available in those days, so the best idea was to find digs. It sounds easy, but you can't just go round knocking on every door in London, asking if people fancied taking in a lodger — even if he was training to be a dentist.

We were very much relying on the help of other people to find something suitable, which led to us receiving some information that was good, some that was bad, and some that was just downright stupid. But, if you don't ask, you'll never find out, I suppose. We did also find out which newspapers and other publications were useful for advertising appropriate accommodation, so, armed with this new knowledge, we set about tracking down my future city-centre penthouse with roof garden and pool (or maybe not).

Mum took me off to London in the car, with the list of names, addresses and so on that we had gathered from a million different sources (or so it felt) and we began checking out the various available digs, an excursion carried out under the instruction from Head Office *aka* Dad, not to return until we found somewhere suitable. There was a proviso. Suitable *and* within budget. Dad's budget.

Needless to say, most of the places we looked at were, shall I say, sadly lacking in some respects. Lacking in hygiene was one of the main observations, but the lacking covered many other aspects as well, such as carpets, furniture, space, light, access...

Speaking of space, it soon became apparent that every landlady or landlord with a spare broom cupboard seemed to think they could rent it out for an exorbitant amount, and call it lodgings. Well, *this* student wasn't having any of that, and neither was Mum — no way could she rest easy back in Manchester, knowing her first-born was working hard and living in a wardrobe.

It was a tricky mission, but eventually we were advised to call on a young family in north west London, who were offering a room in their house as digs. Off we went, by now feeling rather defeated and not really optimistic, so it was a real pleasure to meet this nice young couple with their little four-year-old daughter, Deborah.

The lady of the house showed us round and the room on offer was certainly the best we'd seen so far — by a mile, and we had seen quite a number by this point. As you'd probably guess, the rent was slightly higher than Dad's budget figure, but all it took was Mum and me pleading woefully down the phone to the man holding the purse strings, and it was more than he could handle. He buckled. Budget extended. Room acquired.

Mine, all mine.

More Schooldays

I'm not saying I was the only one, but going straight from grammar school to university, miles from home (therefore, and more importantly, miles from home cooking and proper cleaning) and on my own, was quite a wrench... or maybe a pair of dental pliers.

Skipping over any adverse effects of this emotionally disturbing relocation, it didn't take me long to settle in. Which is just as well, because very soon I felt more *thrown in* than settled in, to the first year of studies covering many aspects of the human physical condition, although not as much as you might expect of actual dentistry. We had to learn all the basics — anatomy, physiology, bio-chemistry, and we were given a teasing glimpse into dental anatomy and dental materials.

Patients, however, there were none. Nil, nada. And so it remained for months on end, to my bitter disappointment.

The Royal, as the Royal Dental Hospital of London was known, was not equipped with the appropriate facilities to accommodate the first-year studies, apart from the minimal dental bits, so we were shipped off to St Bartholomew's Hospital Medical School, near the

Barbican and about two miles from Leicester Square as the crow flies — or any other winged bird that hasn't been partying too heavily. Then, once a week, we would trot back over to the Royal for our dental studies.

Although now, looking back to my time at Bart's, most of it is just a haze, there are three things that I do remember clearly (thank heaven, I was beginning to think it was just a dream).

Remembering the Bodies

To begin, I do remember my very first anatomy lecture.

The person casting his pearls of wisdom to us lowly students was Professor Alexander Cave, who, I later discovered (courtesy of Mr Google), had been born and raised in Manchester and had graduated in medicine from Manchester University. He lived to the ripe old age of 101, and I can't help thinking that, perhaps if he hadn't had to deal with us, he could have made it a bit further.

Most of his audience at that particular lecture were kids who were just out of sixth form at school. In true rebellious schoolboy style, we all made straight for the very back rows of seats in the lecture theatre — obviously, to be as far away from 'the teacher' as possible. It was *de rigueur,* it was what had to be done.

So that's what we did.

And there we sat, until Professor Cave entered the lecture theatre, took his seat at the desk (which now seemed to be quite some distance away) and began to speak.

We couldn't have known that he was a particularly quietly spoken man, and that sitting at the very back like stroppy teenagers was completely the wrong move. We didn't hear anything he said. Not a single word. Oops.

I do hope you won't be shocked when I tell you that, when it came to the second lecture, everyone sat at the front of the theatre. Lesson learned.

***

On to my second memory, which is also anatomy-related.

In those days, dental students (or at least those in London — I can't speak for the rest of the UK because I wasn't there) had to carry out dissection on cadavers. For those of you who are not familiar with the word, a cadaver is a dead body. A dead *human* body. Shall I give you a moment?

For some reason known only to the faculty, we had to dissect most of the body, all except the arms and legs. All other bits — and I mean *all* — had to be dissected. God only knows why this was, when the only part we were going to be even vaguely interested in was the teeth, for goodness' sake, with maybe a little nod to the head and neck.

I understand that, in modern times, due to the difficulty in obtaining cadavers, mainly because body snatching is illegal, even if your name is Burke or Hare, students no longer have the luxury of being able to practise on real human bodies. I imagine they are possibly grateful for this. Instead, they learn from textbooks. Oops! Sorry, I mean they sit at a computer and use the internet. Only those who are going on to become surgeons are bestowed with the privilege of being able to dissect cadavers. At least they don't use live bodies!

After what is now referred to as a 'briefing' in the ante-room at Bart's, we were escorted into the actual dissection room. There, in front of us, tidily arranged on long tables, lay three cadavers (or it could have been four... I can't remember, sorry — maybe when you're suddenly faced with dead bodies, you don't commit everything to memory in a clear and orderly fashion). These dead bodies were covered with crisp, white sheets to protect their dignity, which only added to the strangeness of the situation, believe me.

As we moved towards the table each of us had been allocated, somebody accidentally brushed against the sheet covering one of the bodies. The movement of the fabric caused a movement of what was underneath. Then something flopped out from under the cover, into full view. It was an arm. A human arm, pale-skinned and limp, lifeless (yes, I know, of course it was) and it revealed itself and then just dangled there.

One among us, obviously not as prepared for the sight of a dead person as the rest of us, or maybe having not had a substantial breakfast, couldn't take it. A quick exhale, a wobble, then — flat on the floor, in a dead faint. Gone.

When the poor student was brought round, I wanted so much to say, *It's okay, it's completely 'armless*, but I didn't.

***

And my third recall from that dim and distant era is, again, related to anatomy.

I was staying in my digs in North London with the young couple, Henry and Frances, and their little girl. Their house was quite large and I'm fairly confident their mortgage would have been somewhere in the eye-watering region, so my weekly rent money would have helped out a bit.

The arrangement was that I had a bed-and-breakfast service during the week, then, come the weekend, my dinners (evening meals, in case you are among those of us who believe that dinner is eaten halfway through the day) on Friday, Saturday and Sunday evenings were included. If ever I did want to have dinner with them in the week, all I had to do was tell Frances in the morning (apparently, cooking meals carries with it some level of planning, but how would I have known?) and pay the princely — pre-decimalisation — sum of ten bob. That's ten shillings, and that's now a whacking — post-decimalisation — fifty pence.

The mid-week dinner thing became quite the norm, which was great because I enjoyed their company. The norm, all except for Wednesdays.

On Wednesdays, almost religiously, I gave myself a little treat in the form of a visit to Blooms, a rather famous kosher deli restaurant in Golders Green, an establishment that had already enjoyed half a century of culinary success.

Here, I would enjoy my regular order of bean and barley soup (this dish was the source of the restaurant's fame and popularity), followed by steak and chips. Sometimes, just to prove my eating habits are not boring, I'd have potato latke instead of chips. I know how to mix things up. Oh, yes.

On one non-Wednesday day, I had arranged to eat with Henry and Frances that evening, and no doubt handed over my hard-earned ten bob accordingly. At the hospital that day, we were in the dissection room, working our way down a body, and we arrived at the liver. This organ was duly removed, and even more duly dissected into wee liver slivers.

When I arrived home, ready for one of Frances' special ten-bob dinners, imagine my reaction (especially in the stomach region) when I saw that dinner was, in fact (you'd never have guessed), liver.

I would like to say I never ate liver again, but that would be a lie and I was brought up not to tell lies. It has actually always been (apart from that one particular non-Wednesday day, that is) one of my favourite foods, even if it causes me to put weight on.

Maybe that's poetic justice for all of the livers we took from their rightful owners and cut them into little bits. Who knows?

Feeling Feverish

1967. I was in my first year at university and it was Easter. To be precise, it was Passover.

Instead of a nice big chocolate Easter egg, I got a fever. It did its best to avoid being diagnosed, and, as the symptoms were a sore throat, high temperature and a feeling of total lethargy, it could have been anything from a cold virus to black swamp fever or beri-beri, for all I knew. Still, after a while it disappeared and when Easter was over, I went back to Uni (hopefully minus the beri-beri).

That was obviously tempting Fate, because the symptoms returned — and with a vengeance. I was really ill. And those who sat at the bedsides of the very ill, stethoscopes dangling beneath poker faces (you can never tell by looking at them whether you're almost dead or perfectly healthy), decided it was probably (there's nothing to reassure a person and instil confidence like a 'probably' diagnosis) — as I was saying, they said it could possibly be glandular fever.

Very little was known about this terrible disease at the time, and Bart's was actually researching the condition, not because of me being ill, you understand — I'm not that important. They had a ward crammed with medical students, dental students and nursing students (it wasn't known as the 'kissing disease' for no reason) and it was suggested that I should go there. If I say I ducked out of this opportunity and avoided the place like the proverbial plague, believe me, that's the understatement of the century.

So, off I toddled, with my probably-but-might-not-be illness, back to the comforting bosom of home in Manchester, to be tended and cared for by my mum.

Living next door to the family abode was a very senior paediatrician from the local children's hospital, and he was called upon (why not?) to take a look at the poorly one.

Because I had the sore throat and high temperature, the doctor gave me an injection of antibiotics. For those of you who may aspire to be medically knowledgeable, this was called Penbritin, which is now known as ampicillin, a form of penicillin.

This treatment had absolutely no effect whatsoever on my symptoms, and the fever and sore throat just hung on in there — well, in me. What it *did* do was to elicit a severe allergic reaction, causing rashes over my body and what I can only describe as solid ear lobes, which was, in anyone's opinion, weird. So, what did the good doctor do next? He gave me a second dose!

This extra shot of rash-producing, ear-solidifying antibiotic had equally no effect on whatever was going on in my system, and it transpired that the illustrious paediatrician knew as much about glandular fever as I did. That's one big fat nothing.

Medical literature overflows with advice to this day *not to use ampicillin* if glandular fever is suspected because the reaction as experienced by Yours Truly typifies the presence of the disease. For many years after this, I was convinced I had an allergy to penicillin because of what had happened. Now, I'm just not sure.

One thing I am sure of is — I didn't have beri-beri.

Fishy Fridays

When we students eventually became full-time at the dental hospital, we ate lunch in the refectory (you and I would call it a café or a dining room, but London University at the time had a 'thing' about giving everything fancy names).

This refectory was on the first floor of the building and was divided into two separate areas — the main room was for us students, but behind the serving area and kitchen was a smaller, private dining room for the faculty (that's the teaching staff) accessed by a door at the side of the service area, and this door was kept locked. Each faculty member was given a key to the special dining room, thus ensuring that no *hoi polloi* students could enter the hallowed area.

I never found out if the diners behind that locked door ate the same food as we did, or if perhaps they enjoyed choice dishes from a very different menu. If they did eat the same food as we lesser beings did, what could have been the reason for keeping the room locked, I wonder? It's the kind of situation that sends your mind racing…

Being a non-meat eater, (except for kosher meat, of course) gave me a bit of a problem with these lunches, because, apart from the fish served every Friday, the options were all meat. There was one exception to this, and they hadn't wasted much time or creative energy coming up with it, I assure you. Egg and chips.

So, my lunchtime diet from Monday to Thursday consisted of double fried egg and chips. In a desperate, albeit vain, attempt to liven things up a bit, I devised my (not cunning, not by any stretch of the imagination) plan. On Mondays, I would have my double fried egg and chips with *brown* sauce (and it was the real McCoy, HP); on Tuesdays my double fried egg and chips would have the addition of *tomato* sauce (I'd like to say it was Heinz, but I reckon it would have been the cheaper brand) (I bet they had Heinz in the locked dining room); on Wednesdays I would have double fried egg and chips with — yes! you guessed it — brown sauce; and on Thursdays I had my 'Thursday Surprise' dish of double fried egg and chips... with tomato ketchup.

Thank heaven for Friday! I never thought I'd be so thrilled to see a piece of fish on my lunch plate. And, to add to my delight, it came with mashed potato.

Strict Standards

In today's world, I'm pretty sure that most people (those who visit a dentist at some point, anyway) are familiar with the sight of their dentist in full surgery garb, i.e., wearing a face mask, surgical gloves and dental tunic or clinical scrubs (that's the two-piece outfit that resembles a pair of pyjamas).

It has been said that the white tunic was made famous and immensely popular by a TV series in the early to mid-1960s, called Dr Kildare (and please note, I am not even vaguely interested in such TV programmes — never have been, never will be), in which an actor named Richard Chamberlain pretended to be a doctor but it didn't matter that he couldn't do anything a doctor did, because he was a handsome young man who made young ladies (and many a bit older) swoon at the sight of him. He wore a particularly fashionable tunic top with a sort of Mandarin collar and side fastening. So, now you know.

Just a thought — I wonder if any dentist has ever worn actual PJs that could be mistaken for scrubs and, after accidentally sleeping late one morning, has just thrown on a coat and pair of shoes, grabbed the car keys and zoomed off to their practice, still wearing the PJs.

And, if so, did anybody notice, or make any comment? As I said, just a thought.

Anyway, back in the latter part of the 1960s and into the early '70s, only the dental surgeons who worked in the actual operating theatre and performed dental *surgery* on their patients (and I mean *serious* surgery) wore a face mask and surgical gloves.

We lesser mortals who were excluded from that esteemed category didn't wear anything. Oops! I mean, we didn't wear the gloves or face mask — we were hands-on (literally) with our naked fingers working in the mouths of patients requiring such treatments as tooth fillings, extractions or minor surgery. The other thing we did, in our un-masked and un-gloved state, was to take dental impressions, which could be particularly revolting if the patient puked.

It was quite common for a patient to gag when the impression putty was placed in their mouth, but some just couldn't help literally vomiting. And, when you are hovering, bent forward, just inches (or even less) away from the person about to throw up, you simply don't have time to get out of the way. No matter how many times it happens. And there's me with my life-long aversion to physical sickness. Life can be so unfair.

Something else that's changed drastically since those heady days is the sterilising of our instruments. The equipment used for this process, called a dental autoclave, was in its early infancy at the time — in fact, it was almost embryonic. So, it was only used selectively back then.

The autoclave had been introduced into the fillings department, but not the surgical department! This meant that, in the general anaesthetic operating theatre, where we extracted hundreds — nay, thousands — of teeth under 'sit up' anaesthesia (that's the patient sitting up, not the dentist, in case you're wondering), the method of sterilising the extraction forceps was to — remember, this was a long time ago, before you start scribbling letters to the Health Minister — place them in a metal tray containing an antiseptic solution (for anyone interested, I think this was chlorhexidine) (for those not interested, don't bother reading that last bit).

We were supposed to handle the forceps in this sterilising process by lifting them in and out of the tray using a large pair of tweezers. More often than not, we used our (un-gloved and completely naked) bare hands.

And guess what? We *never* killed anybody. CQC[¥], eat your heart out.

Note: this book is not just incredibly funny, entertaining and interesting — it's educational as well. There will be questions later.

[¥] CQC: Care Quality Commission: the independent regulator of healthcare and adult social care services, ensuring the care provided by hospitals, dentists, ambulances, care homes and homecare agencies meets government standards for quality and safety.

London Tour Guide (*but I won't go south of the river, guv*)

When I first packed my spotted hanky, tied the corners in a knot and hung it on a stick before starting out for The Smoke, The Big City, The Capital — or we can just call it London — this was regarded by northerners as an exotic adventure, a huge and potentially perilous expedition, on a par with being dropped by parachute into the most fearsome and dense area of the Amazon jungle. Most of us didn't normally venture any further south than Sheffield.

In those days, you didn't hop on a 390 Pendolino high-speed electric passenger train and find yourself in London a mere two hours and seven minutes later. Oh, no.

But you did have a choice of transportation for this epic expedition: you could climb aboard a rather slow diesel train (compared with the modern equivalent, 'slow' does not come close to describing it) — not quite the glorious days of steam, but only a little more progressive — and you could purchase lunch aboard, in the form of the famous (infamous) British Rail sandwich, complete with curled corners — or you could drive.

Most of your route would be A roads — some of which were really B roads in places — because the motorways didn't extend to the remote regions of the 'up north' classification. Not yet.

So, as you can imagine, such a trip was a really big event in the life of a northerner and you therefore had to pack in as much as possible of seeing the sights, experiencing those things we'd only ever previously seen on the telly (and possibly thought they were fictional). You know of what I speak — the Palace, (Buckingham, that is — not the theatre), London Bridge, the Tower of London, the Houses of Parliament... and so on. *But,* because you weren't a Londoner (my-be it's becorse Oi'm a Lahndoner...), how would you get around efficiently and in a timely manner, to fit in as many of these as you could? *And,* of course, you didn't have the foggiest clue where any of these places actually were. So, you needed someone to take you on your sightseeing quest, didn't you? And who could that be, I wonder?

Oh, isn't David Cohen living in London now? Maybe he'll show us around.

Tower Bridge by Freddie, aged 8

But, for some reason, these people couldn't pick up the phone and call me with their request. Oh, no, they had to get to me via my parents, who would then arrange the availability of my tour guide duties during our weekly phone chat on a Friday afternoon.

I haven't mentioned this before, but by November 1966, when I'd got settled into my life in the city (looking back, I'm amazed they never made me a Pearly King) my dad, being the great dad he was, bought me my first car. A two-door Morris Minor, registration number VWH 348. This little wheeled wonder had previously belonged to my grandma on my mother's side, who sadly passed away a couple of days before I received my A-level results (so she didn't get to know what a genius her grandson was).

Back to the tour guide part... having been cajoled by my parents to agree to do this, I was to collect the intrepid northern explorers from Euston station — not the salubrious centre of sophistication we see today, where cosmopolitan travellers scurry to and fro endlessly, but the dark, dismal, smoke-blackened Victorian structure, offering no more than cold, characterless waiting rooms and lonely windswept platforms where sad-faced travellers would stand and peer up the line, hoping their train would be on time, to whisk them away from the gloom before depression took hold.

Bear in mind, this tour guiding was done on my afternoon off work, and Euston station would definitely not be on my list of places I would choose to be. If the visitors had already arrived in the city, I would pick them up from their hotel instead.

Remember, back then the traffic, wherever you went, was nowhere near as dense, fast, dangerous or downright annoying as it is now, and you could actually get about by car quite easily (think of the Lake District now, on a very wet — what else would it be? — winter's day, and you've got the picture) — but, as in any big city, you needed to know your way around.

So, off we'd toddle in my little Moggy Minor, usually taking in the sights of the West End, and, of course, one of the highlights of the tour, a visit to Downing Street. Hard to believe now, but then you could drive along the street, stop outside No. 10, take a few photos by the front door, get back in the car, drive up to the end of the road, turn round and drive back along past the PM's abode again. There just wasn't the security we see there now. One lonely bobby on duty, and he'd smile and chat, and there was no problem at all with you being there. But don't mention it to MI5, in case they still have some unresolved issues from back then.

This weekly ritual went on for some months, until I had to return home (to Manchester, not my new home in London), on 'sick leave', the 'sick' part of which, in my case, was glandular fever, as already mentioned. When I was recovered and back in the capital, later in 1967, I was once again nominated tour guide, but this time with an added extra.

In February of that year, a Very Big Thing happened to the Jewish community in the UK — any idea what it was? Yes? No? Okay, I'll put you out of your misery. It was *Fiddler on the Roof* opening at Her Majesty's Theatre on Haymarket. The Israeli actor, Topol, played the lead role, but don't ask me anything else, because that's all I know.

A lady at the dental hospital, known as the Almoner (that was her job title, not her name, although she could have fitted in to any Batman episode along with the Joker, the Penguin and the Fiddler) (that's not the same Fiddler as the one on the roof, by the way) ... anyway, this lady had some obviously excellent contacts in the London theatre scene and she managed to obtain complimentary (yes! absolutely free!) tickets for most of the theatres — including Her Maj's. So, my girlfriend of the time, now my wife of almost 52 years (I know, how has she put up with me for so long?) and I had seen most of the shows we wanted to catch, including *Fiddler on the Roof*.

As a gesture of gratitude for my concerted efforts in schlepping these people around London in my Moggy, some of the visitors thought it would be a great idea to take me to the theatre. Yes, of course, to see *Fiddler on the Roof.* I didn't have the heart (or lack of) to tell them I'd already seen it (how many times? Oh, so many) so I went.

Topol went, too. Not with me, he just left the production and was replaced by Alfie Bass. Then Alfie went, and the part was taken over by another actor, and so on, and so on. By the time I'd seen the performance so many times, I reckon they could have asked me to stand in. For any of the parts — I'm sure I could recite them all.

My role as London Tour Guide was interrupted quite rudely when my beloved grandma's motor car was stolen from outside my flat in Kilburn towards the end of 1967. As you can see, I had raised my profile from lodger, in my digs with Frances and Henry, to the lofty heights of flat dweller.

Strangely, I found myself suddenly reinstated when I discovered my little vehicle as I walked home (well, what else could I do? I had no car, remember?) a few days after the sad loss, to find it parked very neatly just round the corner. And, before you even think it, no! This was *not* a case of me having forgotten where I'd parked it, following a night on the tiles (with a fiddler, perhaps).

These things were quite possible at the time, due to there being no drink-drive laws, but I was not guilty, m'lud.

Morris Minor by Freddie, aged 8

I was overjoyed to have Moggy back. It had been hot-wired and taken for a spin (not as exciting as it sounds in the case of a Morris Minor). I ran back to the flat to get my car key, hoping the car would still be there when I got back. It was! And so, Yours Truly was back in the tour guide industry — a purely honorary post, apart from a ticket for *Fiddler on the Roof.*

Making an Impression

Having touched on the subject of impressions earlier, allow me to delight you with a little of the background to my work in this particular sector of the dental world.

It had come to pass, in October 1967, when I was doing my time at the Royal, that we were finally let loose on actual real human patients. *But,* we weren't allowed to go straight to working on actual real teeth (just in case a lack of experience caused issues that then caused litigation, I guess), and so they gave us those unique members of the patient category known as edentulous patients — they're the ones who had no teeth. Not a one.

'Twas on the fifth floor of the Royal Dental Hospital in Leicester Square in the city of London, fine historic capital of this wonderful country of ours, where I saw my *first ever* patient. A proper live person. I was almost dizzy with the power.

My history-making patient was a gentleman, a bus driver with London Transport, who was in need of a full set of dentures, and who — for whatever reason — was perfectly happy to put his mouth in the hands of Yours Truly, B. David Cohen, dental student extraordinaire.

The first stage of this procedure is to glean the patient's medical status — any symptoms (I suppose in this instance, the over-riding and glaringly obvious symptom would be not having any teeth), any medication being taken, medical history, previous dental treatments (I'm guessing that included extraction of all teeth, unless this chap preferred the more old-fashioned and less sophisticated method of tying string to a doorknob), and so on.

Once this is covered, the second stage is to take an impression of the mouth, from which the dentures will be made. This is not, dear reader, as simple as it may seem. First, I had to mix up the dental putty myself, since it isn't something of which you can say, *here's one I made earlier*. Because it sets and then goes rock hard, and is completely useless as any kind of mould.

I got through the mixing part, placed the resulting soft putty lump in an impression tray, and then proceeded to press it into place in the patient's mouth. Now, all we had to do was wait for it to set solid while the patient lay back in the chair.

Then — WHOOSH! Puke, violently hurled all over me. Mess. Smelly mess. Smelly, sticky, warm, lumpy, revolting mess that had shot out of another human being. On me. It was all I could do, not to be sick myself.

And that was my first impression (yes, please forgive the really bad pun) of clinical dentistry. And I have been plagued by a severe aversion to physical sickness for as long as I can remember — even when my own children were very young and they would be sick at times, I would hurtle from the scene, leaving my poor, long-suffering wife to deal with the resulting problem.

It didn't take me long, believe me, to devise a method of taking an impression without fear of causing the patient to even gag, never mind spew in volcanic proportions, their entire lunch over me.

I believe that is known as self-preservation.

Dental Nurse

It was 1966. While I was waiting for my A-level results, I decided to take advantage of the free time and go on holiday, which turned out to be very fortunate because, while I was away, I met a young lady called Marsha. In 1968, even more fortunately, we got engaged.

Back to normality, I was being treated to the delights of my student placement at the Royal, which included a midweek ritual that was possibly based on the idea that we students required some form of recreation to balance with the lectures and learning. This was, to me, almost a form of torture. Wednesday afternoons, otherwise known as 'sports time'.

All clinical pursuits were put on hold and groups of young men would throw themselves (literally, in some cases) into a game of rugby or football, or whatever testosterone-driven activity they preferred.

Some, of course, being given the freedom to utilise this time playing *any* sport at all, would challenge each other to that famous British form of exercise involving only the forearm and hand. Lifting pints of beer, with the added excitement of each contestant trying to outdo the others by drinking the largest volume of their chosen ale.

I, however, was not even vaguely interested in any or all of the above, and chose the much more sedate game of tennis, partnering in doubles matches with Marsha's aunt. Winter and summer alike, we would play, blatantly flying in the face of Cohen's Rule No. 1, SK *(Sport Kills)*.

And, to prove that I was dead right to *have* this rule, in February 1969, during a game with Auntie Jean *et al*, I turned to run to the baseline to send back a particularly high ball, when — whack! I hit the floor like a felled tree. And I was writhing in sheer agony.

A trip to the local hospital produced a diagnosis of a torn Achilles tendon in my right ankle. And I had to have the offending area covered in Plaster of Paris — not the same plaster as used in the dental lab, but the type that stops you moving about easily. Or moving at all.

What you don't know yet (because I haven't told you) is that, on the third of August that same year, only a few months ahead, I was due to marry Marsha, who was by then my fiancée. The news that I was thus incapacitated did not go down well with her. Nor did it go down well with my family, equally not with my future mother-in-law, and certainly not with my supervisors at dental school. Their silly fault for making me do 'sports time'.

However, not being one to give up easily (otherwise known as stubborn), I somehow managed to get myself into the hospital on a regular basis (please don't ask how, because the mists of time have obscured the memory, and I have a feeling that might be just as well), and I was even able to treat patients.

But, when it came to fetching the materials I needed, which were at the other end of the clinic (much like the TV remote, although completely different animals, dental materials are known for always being at the farthest end of the room from wherever you are), I just couldn't manage that. So, 'the management' allowed me to have the assistance of a dental nurse. This was unheard of at the time, and seen as a real luxury — and this episode of my physical limitation was the only time during my whole four years at the Royal when I had this help. Ever since then, I have never been without at least one dental nurse.

Fortunately (for me, anyway), by August my ankle was healed and I was able to perform the daunting task of walking down the aisle and back up again, without any form of support. As this was deemed to be mandatory, a command issued by my mother-in-law, I was thankful. Oh, so thankful.

In case you're interested (and even if you're not), I still have trouble with that ankle, over fifty years later. I always know it's getting bad when people tell me I look like I'm limping. It's especially bad in cold and wet weather. Living in Manchester, I've got no chance.

Nice Little Earners

So, Marsha and I had met, were engaged and then married, and in 1970 we managed to produce a little person of our own — and all before I qualified. Our parents were helping us out financially with the small rented house in north west London that we called home, and from where I commuted to the dental school in the West End.

My commute was a multi-vehicle operation requiring a high level of organisational and management skills. The first leg of my Monday-to-Friday journey involved me straddling my trusty Honda 50 motorcycle (the machine that was one step up from a moped, embarrassingly), adorned with L-plates because I didn't acquire my full motorcycle licence until much later, when I was in practice. My Honda and I would buzz our way from home to the nearest underground station, where the second leg of the journey commenced with me clambering aboard a tube train to Leicester Square.

As the end of my stint at dental school approached, I had quite a lot of time on my hands, with lectures having finished and my clinical time now limited. Consequently, there was a need for me to enhance my student grant income, and that necessitated taking whatever part-time jobs I could find. Although I had a fair few, only a couple have been embedded in my memory...

Chauffeur. One of those French words that we English adopted to make something seem more sophisticated than it really was. Like saying *café* instead of coffee bar, or *faux pas* instead of cock-up, and so on. Anyway, I became a chauffeur (if you take away the French involvement, it's a posh cab driver, guv) for a luxury chauffeur-driven car hire company that was based near where we lived. It was really a taxi firm, but the drivers had to wear the uniform, including the peaked cap, in line with the bigger cars and no doubt the bigger charges.

This posh cab company had a particular corporate client who provided much regular business. This was one of the Commonwealth's High Commissions, and I remember we spent quite a lot of our time ferrying their senior members around the West End. Remember, this was 1970–71 when traffic in the area (and presumably every other area) was much less than it is now, so parking was somewhat less traumatic. Having said that (because I just did) there were still parking restrictions on many of the major roads.

I particularly recall on several occasions taking a lady from the High Commission for shopping expeditions on Regent Street, where parking was impossible. You'd be amazed at how easy it was for a chauffeur (with the appropriate vehicle, of course, not just standing there on his own) to park *anywhere he chose* as long as he just stood by the car (which was always spotlessly clean and gleaming to the point of causing temporary blindness to innocent passers-by) with his cap under his arm, looking 'official'.

It always amused me when even the policemen and traffic wardens would stop to chat (always commenting on the car, like we men do), and not once did they consider issuing the big, black, shiny limo, and its medium-sized white (and definitely not gleaming) driver with a ticket.

I have kept that chauffeur's cap to this day and sometimes, when I take my wife and her friends to and from the theatre in Manchester, I park on double yellow lines (if the police ask, this is part of the fiction element of the book) and, with my cap under my arm, I stand by the car and wait for Marsha and co. to exit the theatre, to be driven home in style. As I wait, I can see people looking with much curiosity, and I guess they are wondering which famous person the chauffeur-driven car is waiting for!

***

The other job I remember clearly is my time as a postman during the 1970 Christmas rush.

When I was given my 'walk' (the official — if not very creative — name for the postman's round), I was pleasantly surprised to see it included our address.

My sojourn into the world of mail delivery coincided with the national changeover from town gas to natural (not national!) gas, and the road outside our house was being dug up to prepare for this conversion.

One day, when I was delivering the post in the street where we lived and approaching my own house, the workmen had reached the area of road outside our front door. They acknowledged me and I replied with a wave of my hand as I walked up to the door and rang the bell, bringing my wife to open the door. I then stepped inside and the door closed behind me.

Roughly fifteen minutes later, this postman (me, obviously) came out of the house accompanied by the lady (my wife, equally obviously), and gave her a kiss before she closed the door and I walked back into the street to continue my round (sorry, my *walk*).

I wish I'd had a camera. The looks on the faces of those poor gas workmen were a picture — an image worth keeping for posterity.

***

During the summer of 1971, I did a short spell at the post office while the regular postman was on holiday. As before, I was given the *walk* that included our house.

This was well before email and all the other means of communicating via modern technology, and in those dark times of yesteryear when folk went on holiday, they would send postcards (some readers might like to Google that) to family and friends. Normal postcard messages would read, *Arrived safely, B and B is nice, weather good. Wish you were here.*

Although, of course, I never read any of these postcards (as if I could even entertain such an idea), I have to say the humble postman could learn an awful lot about their neighbours from the comments on some of those cards.

I repeat, I *never* read any of them. Not ever, m'lud.

Cohen's Collections

Getting back to why I'm writing this...

Over the years, I've been fortunate in being able to give many lectures on my chosen subject, endodontics. That's root canal treatment to most folk, and yes, I know — ugh.

I began to notice that — inadvertently, of course — I would often (some say too often) intersperse my little anecdotes into said lectures. Some of these would have been relevant to the content of my educational address; others, well, maybe not so much. If they came into my head, I would tell them. Simple.

Eventually — by which I mean forty-odd years later — it dawned on me that I should document these crazy stories and give other people some insight into life on the happy end of the drill. Plus, I could do with getting them off my chest so I could maybe, just maybe, get a decent night's sleep.

It wasn't just being a dentist that attracted the funny tale-inspiring situations: I also gathered quite a collection from my travels, and I've been lucky enough to have visited many foreign lands — and we all know that travelling brings its own anecdotes, as well as a broader mind.

A lot of people collect things. It's not a crime. Not yet. I have quite a collection of miniature spirit bottles, and I don't mean the kind with the wish-granting genie inside, however happy that would make me. Currently, I am the proud owner of three hundred and twenty-four whisky and one hundred and forty-seven vodka bottles. I have also collected three children, six grandchildren and one wife (who will possibly kill me for saying that, just like when I introduced her to someone as 'my first wife').

How about my collection of licences? To date, I have accrued a full driving licence, a motorbike licence, a Private Pilot's Licence, a Boat Captain's Licence, and the Institute of Advanced Motorists certificate (okay, not a licence as such, but I'm counting it). And, of course, my General Dental Council Licence, otherwise known as my licence to drill.

Other collections I can boast are the countries and territories I've visited, currently eighty; the various American states I've been to, twenty-five to date; and the airlines who have had the undoubted pleasure of carting me to and from all of these far-off places, ninety-one. These collections are all neatly stored — not in the attic, but, as this is the twenty-first century, on an Excel spreadsheet. While thinking about all the travelling I've done, somehow my wife seems to have clocked up her own collection of seventy countries visited — that's serious competition.

Whenever I visited a country for the first time, I would buy my daughter a doll dressed in the national dress, and I'm pleased to say she still has all of them. So, not really one of *my* collections, but I did provide it and this is my book so I'm counting that, too.

Some time ago, I discovered there was a club called *The Travelers' Century Club,* the joining requirement for which salubrious clique was that you had travelled to one hundred different countries or territories (put your hand up if you understand the difference). So, that is now my goal, and I only have another twenty to go! Mind you, it's easier said than done just now, with our new friend, Covid-19, hanging around every corner of the globe. One day…

As it happens, while I was writing this, I checked out the proper name of that club, as I cannot possibly be seen to insult them by getting their name wrong when I'm grovelling for membership, now can I? It was then that I spotted their offer of a provisional membership to people who have visited over fifty countries.

Is my application written, sealed in an envelope and posted?

You bet.

The First Interview

In the late 1960s and into the early '70s, as final year dental students approached the end of their course and looked forward to qualifying as registered dentists, they were faced with making a decision as to which career path to follow.

Basically, there were three to choose from:
- Join the armed forces
    Some of the students had already signed up as cadets while attending dental school, and for their magnificent gesture they were paid a handsome stipend on top of their student grant.
- Enter the world of academia (but from the other side of the classroom) and/or become part of the hospital service.
- Go into general dental practice.

If you chose the first option, either during or following graduation, you would have to commit to being in the service for a number of years — you couldn't just dip in and out, like on the *Pick 'n' Mix* counter in Woollies. Long-term commitment wasn't something students liked to think about — too scary. The second option was popular with a number of students, in one of its variations (students, or young people in general, do like choices and variety).

Most of us, however, including Yours Truly, chose general practice, and, as the end of the final term of the final year loomed ever closer, we all started to look for jobs. I'd say probably 99.9% of us became associates in established dental practices.

As I was living with my wife and baby son in London, it seemed sensible for me to find a practice in the London area where I could take my first real steps in my real career as a real dentist.

Easier said than done, dear reader. Thwarted, I was! By the government. In April 1971, having managed since the NHS began in 1948 without changing things, they introduced charges (yes, actual money) in health service dentistry. Would you Adam and Eve it? Just when I'm about to begin my career proper, they go and scare patients away by demanding money!

Prior to this, people would pay a small contribution towards the cost of their treatment, in the princely sum of thirty bob, otherwise known as one pound and ten shillings, which today equates to £1.50. For this amount, patients would receive all of the treatment they needed (dentist's opinion) but maybe not all they wanted (patient's opinion).

This new system obviously had a negative effect on the world of dentistry, in that practices saw less patients, and for less treatment, and the practice owners kept the remaining patients for themselves (not rocket science) so there wasn't enough work (translating to income) to warrant having an associate on board. Like me.

Hence, finding an associateship close to home (home at the time, i.e., London) was an extremely difficult project. As well as location, location, location, I wanted to be in a practice where I was comfortable, and where I'd be happy to work. Not a lot to ask, or so I thought.

I remember one particular interview — I had to travel quite some distance to get to the place — where I was met by the practice principal, with the greeting, *Hello, I'm Mel Gibson* (not really, but I forget his name). *Let me explain to you that in this practice the first thing we discuss with the patient is* — at which point he stopped speaking and leaned forward, his face looming a bit too close for comfort, I thought. He was obviously hoping the dramatic element would add meaning to his words. Sadly, there was only one more word.

Money.

Needless to say, there was no way on earth (or any other planet) I could have worked there. Or with him. As I was leaving the building to walk across the car park, I spotted his car. Actually, you don't just *spot* this car. This car appears like an angel from heaven and insinuates itself into the centre of your gaze, where it mesmerises and enchants you… sorry… where was I? Oh, yes! His car. A low, sleek, curvaceous, gleaming vision, an Aston Martin. My dream car for oh, so long. I wondered if I could possibly dislike this man any more than I did at this moment. Nope. I knew then I'd made the right decision. I clambered into my non-Aston-Martin car and left, and I didn't even look back.

Funny how some things turn out — some years later, I discovered that the Aston-Martin-owning, money-grabbing, conversationally defective, self-important dentist chap had got himself into a real load of trouble — and thank heaven I didn't take the job with him, or I'd most probably have been mixed up in it. Shudder.

He'd been very naughty with his business accounts, and the naughtiness had caught up with him. You can't go round claiming payment twice for the same work on the same patient — it's not allowed! It's called fraud and he was charged with it, tried for it and found guilty of it. For his efforts, he was also struck off the Dental Register. Obviously, a man who didn't do things by halves. So, yes! I had definitely made the right decision.

I gave myself a pat on the back for that — my first major positive decision as a professional dentist. It was only a mental pat, as I couldn't reach to do it physically. We may be closely related to the orang-utan, but I am not one.

After a few months of searching for the right job, my father suggested I try someone he knew, a dentist who used to live next-door-but-one to home (that's the family home in Manchester, not the London one). Of course, his dental practice was in Manchester.

I did approach him (I need a name for him for this book, so let's call him Ernie) and it turned out that his associate was due to leave the practice at the end of the year. And if I wanted the position, it was mine! Wow! Now what? I'm living in London with a wife who was (and still is, cor blimey) a real Londoner, through and through. She had no desire, inclination, intention, aim, plan or anything else that would mean she wanted to move to the north of the country.

I was in an unfortunate position, somewhere between the devil and the deep blue sea, if I remember correctly. Good job offer in the wrong area, no job offers in the right area, and my wife standing firm in her daisy roots in the Smoke. It took a lot of talking, persuading, promising, cajoling, and many other 'ing' words, to finally get my wife to agree to relocate. Phew!

When my results came through (I passed, by the way, in case you wonder) we packed up and moved, lock, stock and baby, *up north.*

My first day as a registered dentist was Tuesday, 4th January, in Ernie's practice — and I had my own nurse, a lady called Angela. My very first patient was a little girl, Mary.

I was on my way, and the rest, as they say, is history.

Soaps, Stars and Celebrities

None of us (and by that, I mean the whole human race, not just dentists) can be, do, or know, everything, and I admit I am one of those people who doesn't follow either the sporting world (the real one, not the virtual games that don't really exist) or — and I definitely don't follow this — the world of TV soaps. It goes without saying, therefore, that I wouldn't recognise a famous sports person or a soap star, even if they were in my surgery chair and our faces were about three inches apart.

It wasn't unusual, given our very up-market and highly regarded practice (what is it they say about self-praise?) for us to have very well-known celebrities and quite famous faces staring up at us from the chair. Not that I ever knew who they were. Or cared, for that matter (as long as their bill was paid!).

One day we received a phone call from the local theatre (the one for dramatic and entertaining performances, not the operating one) asking if we could see someone as a matter of urgency. The patient was a world-famous singer in the pop world and was about to be the star in their upcoming pantomime, but he had suddenly developed a toothache, so could we please see him?

With pleasure, we could, and we did. The star duly arrived, complete with his entourage (do these people ever go anywhere on their own? Bathroom, perhaps?) and was escorted upstairs to our general dentist's surgery.

Meanwhile, on the ground floor (and almost on the actual ground), our receptionist was totally blown away by seeing this chap, given that she had been a lifelong fan of his and she couldn't believe he was *here*, in our practice, *in person*.

When his treatment was done, the object of her adoration came downstairs and through Reception, having the same effect on her all over again. She was swooning and almost fainting, unable to speak properly and even more unable to carry on with her job. We had to send her home in a taxi, a quivering wreck!

When she put herself to bed that night, she was probably *Dreamin'* about her *Bachelor Boy*.

I shall say no more.

***

As many people know, a very well-known and staggeringly popular TV 'soap' is produced here in Manchester (I say 'here' as that's where I live now, in case you were wondering), and it was based, until recently, just around the corner from our practice.

Then the soap's production unit was relocated and, coincidentally, we moved our practice, only to end up being around the corner from each other again, which is sad because I'm not (as mentioned earlier) even vaguely interested in these TV programmes.

A lady turned up at the surgery for emergency treatment one day, all dolled up to the nines (like a dog's dinner, some would say, but it would have to be a very hungry dog indeed in this case). Her clothes were way more extravagant (I really mean *garish*) than we were used to seeing, probably because a visit to the dentist isn't normally seen as a reason to dress up in your fancy dress outfit, and she was wearing *a lot* of make-up. She even wore a wig!

As always, I was clueless as to her identity, either the soap character's name or her real name, and, again, as always, I had to have a member of staff discreetly explain to me who the lady was. And that, dear reader, was one of the leading star actresses in the Manchester-based soap.

Of course, I apologised to her for not having recognised her, explaining that I didn't watch much TV (well, I couldn't say I didn't watch rubbish on TV). In return, she explained that the reason she was so over-dressed and wearing so much make-up was because she had been ready to go on set when her toothache suddenly erupted, so she was dressed for filming, rather than a filling!

And I still, to this day, have no idea who that was.

***

Even more soap…

Sometimes I've actually managed to have a proper conversation with a patient — with real words, not just the incomprehensible noises made without the power of being able to form sounds, that come out of those whose mouths have no choice but to remain wide open at all cost.

One such conversation was with a casually dressed young lady who told me she starred in a TV soap that was based in the Yorkshire Dales. Of course, this was yet another TV production that Yours Truly had never seen, never would see, and knew absolutely zero, zilch, *nothing* about.

To add to her no doubt happily expanding CV of TV acting and appearances, this young lady then said she was about to take part in a TV show called *Dancing on Ice,* something else about which I had not the slightest clue. It's quite tricky, having a one-to-one conversation with someone who thinks you should know about something (because in their head, *everyone* should know) when you are completely blank about the subject and you don't want to hurt their feelings (not sure if that's because I wouldn't want to hurt their feelings or because I liked the idea of having their future dental business).

When I'd finished her treatment, she told me she was feeling very nervous, not just about having to have the dental work, but about embarking on the new venture, which it appears is a TV series where a panel of judges (no doubt more people who others would recognise and know things about, but who would leave me in blissful ignorance of their existence) watch couples trying to perform various dances (proper stuff like the waltz, cha-cha-cha, tango and so on, not just jigging about wildly like nowadays) while skating on ice.

These couples, I am given to understand, consist of one professional skater, and this can be the man or the woman, and one popular TV personality — someone who, although confident and adept in their comfort zone of the pretend world of soaps, might not even have *worn* a pair of ice skates, let alone stood up or moved about in them, and certainly not given a step-perfect performance of a *paso doble*.

The things some people will put themselves through in search of more fame and fortune! Anyway, this young lady was telling me how she was not, for one second, looking forward to being thrown around an ice rink in front of judges who — to keep the viewer ratings up — are known to ridicule, insult and injure (emotionally, not physically) the poor contestants in front of millions of the viewing public.

She was very open about her feelings, and I found her extremely likeable and friendly — not something I would normally have associated with these stars of TV Soapland.

It just goes to show, even I can be wrong... sometimes.

***

On one occasion, a gentleman turned up at the surgery for treatment and I had no idea who he was. Well, why should I? Did he know who I was? But there was something about him that did strike me as a little odd — his skin colour. You could describe it as 'tanned', but it was way beyond that, so very, *very* tanned. Very *orange*.

I had a short chat with him, the same chat I have with all patients before doing my work (give or take a few words — I do like to mix it up a bit), then, as you'd expect, I carried out the treatment. I can't remember exactly what he had done, but I can assure you it was of the dental category.

Once completed, I gave him the obligatory POIG talk (that's Post-Operative Instructions Given, for you non-medical folk), then I did my usual security escort bit, walking the patient back to Reception, so he could perform the most painful part of the whole procedure, as many people describe it. Paying the bill.

As he did so, I couldn't help myself and I glanced at his neck, his ears, his head... my eyes darted around, looking for signs of tan lines, or maybe a slight variation in the strangely orange colour of this man's skin. But everywhere was the same deep orangey-brown tan.

As soon as the patient had left the premises, our receptionist couldn't wait to blurt out, *Don't you know who that was?*

Of course, I didn't, which made her roll her eyes and exhale — her statutory response to my lack of awareness of the *Who's Who* of stage, screen and television. I have no idea why people find it so exasperating, but they do.

She explained to me that he was the *very* well-known host of the *very* popular TV series about antiques. It meant nothing to me, as always, but I did wonder how this chap had acquired his strange colour.

And, more to the point, *why.*

Men of Means (*and women, too*)

On the subject of wealthy patients, I'm reminded of a couple of chaps who were well known for their towering presence in the national business scenario.

I was working in a practice in the centre of Manchester, it was the mid-1980s and I was treating them both at roughly the same time. I don't mean they both came into the surgery and sat in two chairs while I stood between them, working on one with my left hand and the other with my right. Although, come to think of it, that is an interesting idea and would have a very positive effect on my income.

The first of these two was, quite honestly, one of the most nervous patients I have ever treated. Weighing in at more than fifteen stone and built like the proverbial brick outhouse, he was one of the toughest businessmen around at the time. But, like all of us humans, he had his Achilles heel — he was scared (and I mean *terrified*) of having any dental work done. I would add that his fear didn't extend to the dentist personally, just the treatment.

Unfortunately, I cannot provide you, dear reader, with any further details, as it would almost certainly give away his identity, and I really would not want to be sued by him. Or, for that matter, by anyone else.

Anyway, he needed some root treatment on a back tooth (upper, if you must know — seriously, you are *so* nosy) and he was insisting on having sedation before treatment.

No problem, I heard myself say, and I sounded nicely confident. *I can do that for you.*

I gave him all the instructions we have to give to patients who are about to undergo sedation: he must have someone with him when he attends for the treatment, so they can drive him home; he must not, under any circumstances, drive any vehicle for at least twenty-four hours after the appointment — this is for various reasons, but one to note is that any vehicle insurance is automatically null and void for twenty- four hours following any sedation.

The day arrived and when he turned up at the surgery, I checked that he had followed all of the instructions, and that he did have someone to take him home. He told me his wife was with him and that she would be doing the driving.

To describe what followed as having a patient who was difficult to treat is a gross understatement. To this day, he holds the record for the amount of intravenous sedation I have ever had to inject into a patient — and yet he still carried on berating me about how unhappy he was because he insisted it wasn't having any effect!

I eventually completed the work and brought him round from the sedation — that was actually a lot easier than normal, because the drugs hadn't affected him in the way I would have preferred, even though he'd been given enough to topple a rhino.

Once we were happy that he had recovered fully, we went through the dos and don'ts with him and his wife, and off they went.

Half an hour later, I had a message to say the patient was on the phone, asking to speak to me. This wasn't unusual because people would sometimes forget to ask about something before they left, and so I took the call. This was in the times before mobile phones, and only some very select (roughly translated, that means extremely wealthy) people had car phones. This chap was one of that elite sector, and his voice came down the line from his open-top Rolls-Royce motor car…

David, he said calmly, *I'm just driving down Deansgate and I've noticed I'm swerving all over the place — is that normal after sedation?*

NORMAL? I screamed back down the line to the Rolls, *I told you NOT TO DRIVE for twenty-four hours!*

I could feel my body preparing for what would be a first massive panic attack as I shrieked the words, and I could hear traffic sounds so I knew his car was actually travelling.

Just before I would possibly have passed out, his voice came back. *Only kidding! My wife's driving, but I thought that was a great joke!*

JOKE? JOKE? I could have quite happily chased this man down Deansgate and dragged him unceremoniously from his expensive car and... well, I would have, if he wasn't so big... and tough... and scary...

***

The other chap was exactly the opposite. He was totally laid back and not at all worried about having treatment, and he was a regular patient of one of my colleagues in the practice.

One day, this chap asked me if I could work my magic (yes, I really do that) with some root treatment to save one of his front teeth. Checking his X-ray did nothing to inspire me with confidence about the possibility of treatment — there was very little bone around the tooth, and it was already so loose, it was wobbling in a light breeze.

My response was simple.

No chance, I told him politely, *it won't work and I think the tooth should be extracted.*

I'm not having it out, and I need you to save it.

I can't save it because it's too far gone.

Look, he said, giving me some serious eye contact, *go into the staff room, have a quiet sit down with a cup of tea, and don't come back until you've worked out how to save my tooth.*

Like a schoolboy who'd just been told to go and sit outside the Head's office, I toddled off to the staff room, wondering why I'd just experienced this strange shift in my professional life, where I now felt like the patient and this chap was behaving like the consultant.

On any normal day in the dental world, the dentist tells the patient to go home and think about the options they have been given, talk to his or her partner, spouse, parent, bank manager, dog, budgie *et al*, then let us know their decision (the patient's decision, that is, not the budgie's). Being told by my patient to go away and think about the treatment was a really weird experience.

Still, that's what I did, weird or not. After a while, I went back to the surgery and spoke to the patient.

Look, I've come up with an idea that could work, but it might not, and IT WILL COST YOU.

I thought if I spoke to him in capital letters, he'd take me more seriously.

How much?

I can't remember exactly what I said, but my guess is that I didn't give a high enough price. This would have been brought on by what I call 'mental-verbal drag' — a serious condition that causes a person's mouth to operate independently of that person's brain, whereas my brain should have come up with an amount of money that my mouth should then have spoken. Instead, however, my mouth decided to give the patient a special offer of fifty per cent off the normal cost.

Oh, that's OK, he relaxed and leaned back in his chair (which tells me it definitely wasn't enough), *I'll just have to give my favourite restaurant a miss for one night!*

How the other half live! Or, in his case, how they enjoy their quail's eggs and foie gras.

Anyway, he had the treatment and — to my enormous (I mean really huge, massive) relief — it worked. I still see this chap from time to time and, as far as I can see, the tooth appears to have survived the thirty-five years that have gone by — including all of the expensive dinners he no doubt shovelled past it. To be honest, I would never ask him about it — too scared!

Strangely, this experience had a profound and positive (and possibly some other adjectives beginning with 'p') effect on my dentistry. Instead of always taking the textbook route, it taught me to look at things differently, to weigh up all angles.

To this day, as long as the patient is amenable, I will always make every effort to save a tooth — if the means of such saving falls within the realms of human possibility (if I may assume you accept that we dentists are, in fact, human). Although today we live in a world where dentists perform successful implants to replace lost teeth, I still tell patients that the best implant in that same world is the root of their own tooth.

The other side of the wealthy client coin showed itself once, when a lady patient came to me for root treatment, also on a front tooth. When she was in the chair and ready for me to begin, she asked me, very nervously, if the treatment was on the NHS, and it was clear to me that she expected the answer to be a resounding *yes*. Unfortunately for her, I had to give her a *no* (resounding or otherwise) and explain that I only carried out this type of work privately.

How much will it cost? she asked, even more nervously.

The standard fee is £100, I replied, not the slightest bit nervously.

I can't afford that much money! That's what we spend on our summer holidays!

How do you manage a holiday for £100?

As soon as I'd said the words, I felt bad — I must have sounded snobbish, facetious, judgemental, and possibly a few other things I wouldn't want folk to think I was.

She spoke quietly. *We go camping.*

I felt thoroughly ashamed of myself.

The lady didn't have the treatment, and ever since then I have felt guilty for not doing the work *pro bono* to make up for what was nothing short of my arrogance.

What's more, I never again commented on a patient's ability, or inability, to pay for treatment — I know nothing about their circumstances or their priorities, and everyone's life is different.

Vive la difference!

The Road to Specialisation

I'm often asked why I decided to change to specialist endodontic practice. I remember it well...

I had been in general practice for close on five years, and, as far as I recall, I was enjoying being a dentist.

However, at the time I was the Honorary Secretary of our local Jewish Dental Society, and it was my job to invite guest speakers to the regular meetings we held in the homes of our members. On Thursday the seventh of October 1976 (a date which I later established to be correct, due to my esteemed position allowing me access to the Minutes of all meetings), I had invited an 'endodontist' from London to speak at our next meeting. Let's call him Maurice (because that was his name, so it's as good a reason as any) and the title we gave Maurice for his talk was *Molar Endodontics*, and to this day I remember his opening words...

I don't know why I've been asked to talk about molar endodontics because, as far as I'm concerned, there is only endodontics, and it doesn't matter which tooth it is being carried out on.

Maurice went on to illustrate the type of endodontics he was performing (at one point he even name-dropped that he had treated a member of the Royal Family, which might be construed as treason in some circles) and the quality of his work was truly astounding.

I may, or may not, have mentioned elsewhere that, when you graduated from London University as a dentist, you did so under the (massive and completely incorrect) illusion that you knew everything and there was nothing more to learn. Not a single word. There was a saying about students who graduated from Guy's, one of the London dental schools: *You can always tell a Guy's man — but not a lot!*

I realised that day that I knew nothing, not a scrap of information, about endodontics, and this was my Eureka! moment. I decided then — this was what I wanted to do.

A few days after the meeting, I wrote to Maurice to thank him for his talk — of course, because (a) I am polite and (b) he had done it free of charge. The other reason for my polite communication was to tell him that his words had inspired me towards endodontics, and to ask if he could possibly recommend any suitable reading matter from which I might begin to develop my knowledge of the subject.

Maurice replied and did, in fact, proffer a suggestion in the form of a book entitled *Clinical Endodontics — A Manual of Scientific Endodontics* by *Sommer Ostrander & Crowley,* which turned out to be (in my then humble and non-expert opinion) one of the worst textbooks on the subject ever written, engraved, carved in stone or drawn on a cave wall.

This left me wondering why Maurice had recommended it in the first place. I did come to realise that maybe he was trying to put me off the specialism for some reason (couldn't bear the idea of stiff competition?), or, possibly more realistically, he was (psychologically) showing me just how difficult it could be as a potential career path.

Nonetheless, it didn't put me off my intended road ahead and, as I continued my studies of the subject, it became crystal clear to me that I really did want to specialise in endodontics. So, how to do this?

In those days, the UK was well behind the US (surprising, when K comes before S in the alphabet) in both dental specialisation and endodontic research. The only 'recognised' specialist areas in the UK were orthodontics and oral surgery (I don't mean talking about surgery, I mean surgery in the mouth).

General dental practitioners were happy to refer patients for orthodontics and wisdom tooth extraction, but felt they could do everything else themselves. I realised quite early on (being the bright spark I am) that general practitioners certainly couldn't perform endodontics as well as it could be done — because either they didn't know there was 'better', or they just felt they were totally capable of the work themselves.

By the end of 1977, I had come to the conclusion that there were two routes open to me, through which I could further my knowledge and acquire skills in endodontics. One was to take up courses in the States. The other was to ask the local dental school if I could work there one or two days a week (unpaid, however that might irk) to treat patients who had been referred for endodontic treatments.

The American Route (pronounced *rowt*, of course). The only post-graduate courses I could find were in the US, and they involved a minimum of two years' full-time attendance. I was offered a place at Harvard University (yes, *that* Harvard) in Boston, but, with three young children, two of whom were in private education (the third was still below school age, in case you think I was being selective about the education of my offspring), there was no way I could afford to move the family to the States for two years.

Then, a dentist friend, Alan (yes, real name — I don't know why you're even querying it), suggested I look in the *American Journal of Endodontics* for part-time courses. I did, and was amazed — and more than a little pleased — to find dozens and dozens of such courses all over the US.

But how would I choose which ones? In the end, I decided to use the old-fashioned method — close your eyes and stick a pin in the page. I did, and I booked myself on the course that had just been attacked by my pin. All sorted, for March 1978.

You need to know that, by this time, Freddie Laker, he of the Skytrain fame and fortune begun in 1977, was making transatlantic flights more and more affordable to more and more travellers. So, it is true that, for my specialist career in endodontics, I am indebted to both Maurice and Freddie Laker.

Then, luck (or fate?) intervened — or maybe just some friends of mine who persuaded me to join them on a rather special holiday, the timing of which coincided slap-bang with this course I'd booked. Course cancelled, pin poised, eyes closed, and another course was duly selected.

As it turned out, this was the best thing that could have happened because the second course was in Boston and it was presented by (a drum roll here would be appropriate) Dr Herbert Schilder, known to some people as Herb, but not those who had a desire to carry on living.

Schilder was one of the great-grandfathers of endodontics. I booked my flights and a place on the course, but when it came to getting a hotel in Boston, they all seemed to be fully booked. I ended up with a cheap hotel that definitely wasn't five-star but it was probably one step up from a park bench (hopefully).

Bear in mind, this was my first ever trip to America! Exciting times! I flew to London then on to Boston in the US of A, and jumped in a taxi (oops! memo to self — speak the lingo, it's a *cab*) at the airport and asked the driver to take me to said hotel. As Boston airport is very close to the city centre, these cab drivers didn't stand to earn a fortune on the airport runs. With a sort of sideways glance in my direction, he dropped me off outside a really seedy-looking building in a really, *really* seedy-looking district. Gulp. But I'd already paid my ten dollars for the room, so in I went. The bedroom could best be described as basic — let's leave it at that.

I did have some contacts in Boston, thanks to my connections through the Jewish Dental Society — in particular, a chap called Joel Dunsky (yes), an endodontist who became a great friend, so I called him to say I'd arrived and would he mind if I came to his practice to observe how American endodontics was carried out.

Joel asked me where I was staying and when I told him, he almost had an apoplectic fit!

You can't stay there! Get out immediately!

Of course, I told him I'd already paid and that my travel agent hadn't been able to find anything else at all in Boston…

Forget the ten dollars! Grab your things, get a cab (I knew he meant a taxi) *to my place and I'll find you somewhere!*

So, I did.

When I arrived, Joel told me the hotel I'd very nearly stayed in was in what was then known as the *Combat Zone* and he said he couldn't think of a worse place for a nice Jewish boy to stay in the whole of Boston. He said, not only was it not safe to walk around there at night, it wasn't safe to walk around in the daytime, either. Thankfully, Joel found a decent hotel for me and for that, I am eternally grateful.

Some years later, I took my wife to Boston to show her the places I'd visited and stayed in, while working through my endodontics education. Believe it or not, the agent booked us into a hotel in — wait for it — yes, the *Combat Zone*! But, as happens with many run-down urban areas, it had been re-developed and was reborn as a tourist area, complete with up-market residential properties and hotels. Talk about a transformation!

And so, my postgraduate endodontic education began under the watchful eye of Herb (actually, he watched me with both eyes). I can call him Herb now because (a) that was his name, and (b) he's dead.

Because of commitments at home, the only way I could pursue my new career strategy would be to attend short courses, and many of them.

I found out quite early on that I had a first cousin once removed (that's my mother's first cousin, which I learned from studying the family tree and a little genealogy) about my age, living just outside Boston. We used to get together in the city on my final day of a course, and spend a bit of time together before I flew home.

On one occasion, this turned into a bit of a nightmare. We were having tea (yes, tea in Boston, I know) in the lounge of my hotel, until I needed to leave for the airport. Being busy chatting, we didn't notice the tall building opposite gradually fade into a gloom and finally disappear from sight, due to a heavy fog coming down.

As I said earlier, the airport in Boston is near the city centre, and it suddenly dawned on me that, if the fog was thickening in the downtown area, then it would certainly be doing similar at the airport. And flights would be cancelled. Remember, no mobile phones then, so no way of calling the airline to find anything out.

I think I forgot to mention that my wife was due to give birth to our third child *that week,* and I needed (on pain of death or something very much like it) to be back home for the event. My cousin and her husband decided, because they knew the area so well and could therefore presumably drive without being able to see more than two feet ahead, that they would take me to the airport and wait with me to make sure I got a flight — preferably to the UK.

One pretty hair-raising car ride later, I'm in the BA terminal listening to the airline staff announce — with a fitting amount of sympathy in their voices — that, due to the fog, their next incoming flight (the plane on which Yours Truly was hoping — praying — to get home) couldn't land at Boston and had been diverted. No other flights available.

Plan B took immediate effect, which necessitated cousin and hubby rushing me to the Pan Am terminal, only to discover the situation there was the same (same city, same airport, same fog). Flights unable to land, being diverted, and a complete lack of other flights.

By now, as well as feeling panicky, sweaty and nauseous with all the rushing around and the ever-thickening fog, I was also starting to 'hear' my wife's voice as she screamed abuse at me for missing the birth of our new baby — the kind of words only a woman in labour (not the political party, the other thing that's definitely *not* a party) can get away with.

More dashing, this time to the TWA terminal. Third time lucky, obviously, and the ticket agent's voice was music to my ears (in stark contrast to the imagined abuse).

Yes, sir, there is a plane going to England, but there's only one seat left.

One seat! That's all I need! I sort of screamed.

Problem solved, abuse averted (hopefully) and life absolutely and definitely saved. Exhale. I thanked my cousin and her husband and let them go, to claw their way back home through the pea soup.

I did make it in time for the happy event, but I did have to accept some (shall we say, *minor*) punishment.

How could you let it get so close to the birth? is one of the few reactions I can put in print.

That baby was a boy, now a man in his forties with a beautiful wife and three amazing children, half of our complement of six grandchildren. Happy families.

The UK Route (pronounced *root*, not *rowt*, FYI)
As you already know, I'd had the idea (I do have them sometimes, whatever you may have heard) of asking the local dental school if I could work, unpaid, with their

patients who had been referred for endodontic treatment.

A senior dentist at the school (let's call him John, whatever his name was) had a strong interest in endodontics, although he wasn't recognised as a specialist, so I chose to address my request to him, assuming he would be more likely to be open to my idea. I didn't find out if he was, or if he wasn't, because I never heard from him. Rude.

Sometime later (could be weeks, could be months, years — I can't remember) when I was attending a conference in the Lake District, I was discussing this with colleagues at the bar, and — would you believe it? — I was only talking to the very person I'd written to (I don't mean he was the only one there — that would have been a really badly organised conference).

It turned out that John had been prevented from replying to me by his boss, on the basis that me doing the work for free would be seen as taking the job from someone who would be paid to do it, and 'the unions' wouldn't like that. As I remember it, the unions didn't like very much at all, and I didn't want to be on the receiving end of their wrath.

However, fate, or something else (but not the unions) was on my side, because a couple of my colleagues had persuaded the dental school to offer part-time MSc courses based on research, rather than didactic training (in case you're interested, that degree would now be an MPhil, with the MSc being reserved for didactic-trained students).

As a result of this stroke of luck/fate/coincidence, John and I agreed that I could enrol as a part-time MSc student, and carry out research in the endodontics field. I started in September, 1981, spending one day a week on some area of research in the lab, with a view to presenting a thesis to the University for the award of an MSc degree.

This latest step in my career came as a bit (actually, a lot) of a surprise to the family, because of my absolutely unshakeable statement in 1971 when I qualified, that I never, *ever* wanted to see another textbook *as long as I lived*. And here I was, back at university — and entirely of my own volition. It seems that *absolutely* and *unshakeably* only last as long as you want them to.

On my first day, John told me he had made a decision that would turn out to be one of the most profound 'game changers' of my life.

Although we had agreed that John would be my supervisor for the degree, and most of the research would be lab-based, he'd had a re-think and selected someone else to be joint supervisor (no, not in charge of the Sunday roast). John took me to meet the head of the dental materials department — we'll call him Edward, regardless of any name his parents may or may not have given him — and Edward wasn't a dentist, but a very highly qualified organic chemist and materials scientist.

He was also a deeply devout Christian. And Edward was to be my joint supervisor.

Between the three of us, we agreed on my research project — I can hear you sigh, so I won't go into detail — but, because it would be lab-based, most of my time would be spent in the lab (surprise, surprise), the library (remember, no internet, just books and lots of them) or with Edward. This led to a really solid friendship between me and Edward, but now I only see him twice a year for lunch because he was appointed a full Professor in the USA. And yes, it's a long way to go for lunch.

Among the other students from around the world, working in Edward's lab on their MSc or PhD research, there were some from Arab countries, and with me being Jewish (yes, I really am), Edward saw potential conflict. So, on day one in the lab, he announced that we would all work together harmoniously and if there was the slightest sign of conflict or racism, the instigator would be excluded immediately.

I have to say, over the next few years we *did* work together in harmony, and we all wondered why there had to be so much conflict in the world (please do not send your suggestions about this to me — send them to world leaders, politicians… anyone, but not me). The harmoniousness was so successful, I even tried their strong Turkish coffee, lovingly brewed in a tin over a Bunsen burner.

The next three years saw me carrying out a lot of lab investigations related to endodontics. Again, I sense the potential for boredom on your part, so I won't go into the technical details, but suffice it to say, in 1984 I had enough material to submit one beautifully bound thesis of 153 pages exactly, to the University.

The requirement was for the student to submit two copies of the thesis, and, of course, the student (in this case, Yours Truly) would like a copy, so it was the norm to produce three copies.

And here's the historical technology bit (or maybe hysterical?). Traditionally, all three copies were produced by typing on a manual typewriter. Manual, as in, it had *no* power, *no* technology, *no* clever stuff, just metal keys on metal arms that bashed metal letter blocks on to an inked ribbon that in turn made an impression on a sheet of paper. Definitely hysterical, and laborious... oh, so l-a-b-o-r-i-o-u-s.

And, if you needed copies (which I did, as I just explained), you had to use three sheets of paper together with two sheets of carbon paper between them. I won't even try to explain what you had to do, should you need to correct a typing error. Just take it from me, it was not something you wished to repeat, once you'd experienced it.

Fortunately, by 1984, the early computers were beginning to get a foothold (or maybe a byte hold?) and I was able to type my thesis this time on — wait for it — a Sinclair Spectrum 64K (check it out and prepare to be impressed). This marvel of '80s technology had no internal memory, so everything was stored on a cassette tape in an external tape recorder.

Another pre-technology-age issue was that modern office printers hadn't been invented yet, and I had to submit the early drafts of my thesis to my supervisors by way of a small thermal printer, the appearance of which was similar to today's credit card machines, which printed out on to little reels of white paper. It almost felt like you were handing your work to these highly regarded professionals on a loo roll.

Having a touch of OCD in my repertoire, and these documents being the sum total of many, many hours of work and note-making, I was always fearful of losing my data, so I would make extra copies of the tapes and then keep them separately in different (often secret) locations.

When I had *eventually* completed the writing and typing of the tome, it then had to be printed — not as a draft this time on a loo roll machine, but properly on A4 paper. The only means of doing this available to Yours Truly was in the form of a Golfball typewriter that could be connected to my 'computer', and, just to add to the already vastly time-consuming process, it only took one sheet of paper at a time… four hundred and fifty-nine pieces of paper later, I had the three copies of my precious (and, with each painful stage of production, becoming ever more so) thesis. I could almost have completed another degree in the time it took!

The printed A4 sheets were duly taken to a bookbinder and a few days later (yes, days — this was a time when we had time to do things) I was the proud owner of three neatly bound copies of my work. As far as I am aware, mine was the first computer-produced document submitted to Manchester University — it was certainly the first with justified text!

I'm wondering, having just talked (all right, pedantic ones — *written*) about so much of the history (albeit recent) of document production that will be totally unfamiliar to the younger readers, will Google actually crash under the pressure of everyone checking out all of the above items and processes from its archives? It is all there, I assure you.

As mentioned, an external examiner is someone whose expertise is in the same field as the research being presented. Because I was working in a limited field of dentistry, the choice of said examiner was equally limited, and it was inevitable that I would know this person. And I did.

As well as reading the thesis, an examiner also had the option to arrange a *viva* with the candidate if he/she (the examiner, not the candidate) thought it necessary to glean further information. A *viva* is effectively a face-to-face interrogation, but I bet they saw it as an interview.

At the time, I was very active in the British Endodontic Society and had risen to the dizzy heights and lofty rank of Treasurer. Included in our organisation were representatives from other related dental societies, one of whom was (you'd never have guessed) my external examiner.

One day, I was at a management meeting in London, and when the meeting finished, all the out-of-towners (who outnumbered the in-towners, making a mockery of these 'national' organisations constantly holding all meetings in London) needed to get back to whichever railway station to catch their trains home. There seemed to be a shortage of taxis (yes, in London — shocking!) and we were all running late, of course, so my external examiner and I shared one. While travelling together, I asked him if he'd received my thesis. Yes, he had, and he'd read it. Then he asked me if I wanted to have a viva.

Not particularly, thank you very much.

Okay.

The taxi dropped me off first, so I said goodbye and left him to pay the fare. Maybe not the most tactful thing to do, but I have to tell you the money was later refunded to the examiner — by the Treasurer, i.e., *me*. So, no bribe there, then.

I received my degree on the thirteenth of December, 1984.

Beyond the Pond

You've just read of my first ever trip to America, unless you're skipping bits of this book, in which case, stop that! — you don't know what you're missing. And now you can learn of my other trips to various places in the USA...

***

I once had occasion to fly to Los Angeles to attend a post-graduate meeting, and I was fortunate to have relatives who lived there, so they let me stay with them for a couple of days before the event. I made the most of my time by preparing for the meeting, which loosely translates to relaxing in the Californian sunshine.

The meeting wasn't actually in Los Angeles (we're not hippies, you know), but in a town some distance away, so I drove there and took a hotel room for the night (I didn't really take the hotel room anywhere — way too big to move and certainly wouldn't have gone in my rental car). Even though I am a Mancunian, I wasn't prepared for what greeted me when I woke the following morning — the temperature had dropped drastically and the rain was coming down in sheets.

So, there I am in sunny California, with my light summer wardrobe and not a raincoat or a pair of wellies in sight. By the time I got to the university, the car park was so flooded it was more suited to parking boats than cars. Just getting out of the vehicle left me completely drenched, right down to my waterlogged canvas shoes.

The professor at the Institute where the meeting was taking place had recently invented a never-before-seen novel dental material, specifically for use in my specialist field. He offered everyone a sample of this stuff that we could take home with us, in return for (there's always a catch) a donation to the charity arm of the American Association of Endodontists.

I handed over some of my hard-earned and he duly gave me a little container that he'd filled with the mystery substance. For those of you sufficiently mature, this container was actually a black plastic cylinder, about the size of a small salt shaker, that would have originally housed a reel of 35mm photographic film. Ah, the good old days...

Well, this material was soon a resounding success in the dental world, and to buy the amount he'd given me would have cost a packet, an arm and a leg, and all of those other phrases that mean a heck of a lot of wonga. *And,* I had enough of the stuff to last me — well, as long as I needed it. Indeed, a lifetime (as long as that lifetime wasn't suddenly terminated by a number seventeen bus). *And,* if I may brag for a moment, I was the first person in the UK to use it.

Just one thing... in 2001 — the second of October, to be precise — while I was working with my old friend and colleague, Phil, our practice burned down. To the ground. All gone. And where was my precious little canister of this magic material that was worth a fortune and would have lasted me forever?

Yes, it was.

***

1847. July twenty-fourth, a pioneering band of Mormons walked all the way from Chicago to a salt flats area in Utah, looking for somewhere to settle where they could practise their religion as members of the Church of Jesus Christ of Latter-Day Saints, without fear of persecution, to which they had been subjected in bucketloads by the not-very-tolerant folks in Chicago (*Chicago, what a wonderful town*) (I'm not going to get that old song out of my head now). They founded Salt Lake City and began building their Temple.

The 1970s. Can't remember when. A lone dentist (Yours Truly) visited Salt Lake City. I didn't walk — I flew by jet plane. I wasn't looking for somewhere to settle, I was looking for a computer software company that was based there, who were offering (for sale, not as a free gift) a computer management system specifically designed for dental practices. Computer systems were still very much in the development stages and we (that's not the royal 'we', it's my work colleagues and me) were trying to computerise the practice and there wasn't anything available in the UK at the time that could meet our specialist business needs.

While I was there, I visited the Temple, but I had nothing to do with building it. From memory, I don't think I was being persecuted by anyone, and certainly not anyone from Chicago.

It was a Sunday afternoon when I arrived and, this being a largely Mormon city, most of the restaurants were closed, which was a bit annoying because the very accommodating software company representative who met me at the airport and was showing me around the city was offering to take me for dinner.

He was very proud of the place and was telling me the history (basically, see paragraph one), explaining that the Temple was the oldest building in the city, having been built with blocks of granite that had to be hauled, one at a time by ox-drawn cart, from the canyon. I could say it's a magnificent building, really impressive. Okay, I will. It's a magnificent building, really impressive.

Mormon Temple by Freddie, aged 8

I asked in what year the Temple had been constructed and he told me — with obvious delight because this was a real piece of local history — 1853 marked the beginning of the work and it was completed by the placing of the capstone in 1892. He was beaming.

I told him our practice building in Manchester was older than that. In an instant, this beaming, happy chappy looked like the bottom had fallen out of his world and he'd lost the will to live. And it wasn't as if I could take back what I'd said.

Oh, dear, not a brilliant day for Anglo-American relations.

***

This was one of my early visits to the US, before I grew accustomed to the vast differences between them (in the States) and us (in dear old Blighty).

The very size of the places, the buildings, the structures — it can be quite daunting to begin with (or just downright terrifying), and Yours Truly was definitely a beginner.

And the traffic! In the cities and large towns, it was unbelievable, with multiple lanes (a much bigger multiple than our three or four), traffic lights everywhere, showing different colours for different lanes, and — worst of all — driving on the wrong side of the road while sitting on the wrong side of the car.

For anybody who has driven abroad in a busy area, the experience of turning at a junction when you and your vehicle are on the other side of the road — and, (just to emphasise the trauma), to make matters worse, you are sitting on the other side of the car — is a heart-stopping adventure in itself.

There was something else. It was scary, and it should have been approached in stages, baby steps, very gradually. The size of the vehicles. I mean the S-I-Z-E! Remember, this was some years ago, when the Americans seemed to love driving something that appeared big enough to live in. With a family of five. And a big dog. Or a pony. Or both. These cars were *huge. Massive. Brobdingnagian* (look it up).

So, I was staying with a friend (also a dentist) in New York when I found out there was a problem with my airline ticket for my flight back home. May I remind you, there was no technology to help deal with such matters, and the only way to resolve this problem (or any other problem — but only to do with flying, not like your cat hurt his paw, that would be silly) was for me to go in person to the airport and speak to the airline personnel. Remember that? Speaking? To another person, face to face? That's how long ago this was.

As I had less than no idea where Kennedy Airport was, or how to get there, my friend said I could use his car for the day, which, if you think about it, is a bit like telling someone you've lost the use of both feet and they give you a pair of trainers. But I accepted his kind offer, since I was running somewhat low on options.

Then, worryingly, we had to get him to work first (worrying for me, not for him — he was pretty much used to going to work). And where was his workplace? Downtown Manhattan. The centre of Manhattan. In this pulsating hive of over-activity, the traffic was — well, you couldn't even call it traffic. It was a mass of moving metal in what seemed like a hundred different lanes, lights flashing everywhere, Walk! Don't Walk! signs constantly changing and people milling across roads, heaving crowds of human beings, horns blasting, engines thrashing… nightmare. If not your worst one, it should certainly feature in the top three.

My friend drove us to his office, jumped out of the car (I use the word *car* loosely, as I've seen smaller double-deckers), threw me the key and smiled a cheery *See you later!*

Then he was gone.

I was on my own. Alone to face the tumult of New York, driving this Oldsmobile I'd never driven before, that took up about the same space as an ocean-going oil tanker, sitting on the wrong side of this car-bus, on the wrong side of the road, with not a flicker of a clue how to get to the airport. All going well so far, then.

Somehow, the metal beast and I made it to our destination. And still both in one piece — bonus. Then I had to park. Easier said than done. In my attempt, I managed to end up on the wrong side of the road — which to me was the right side — just missing out on a nasty accident by the skin of my teeth.

My first experience of driving a left-hand drive car on the right (wrong) side of the road, in an area that was the equivalent of a giant helter-skelter. And I lived to tell the tale. Which I just did.

***

Over Christmas and New Year, 1978, there was a dental conference that I was interested in, and we decided to go as a family, taking the opportunity to have a 'summer holiday' type holiday in the sun — because this conference was taking place in Florida. Orlando, to be exact, so it was the perfect place to take our two older children.

Or, so we thought...

We arrived in Florida to find it was taking a battering (and not putting up much of a fight) from the worst weather the area had experienced in decades, both in terms of temperature, which was bitterly cold, polar, verging on glacial, and the conditions — basically pouring rain, torrential water, floods.

As you'd imagine, having set off to enjoy our break in the sunshine, we had only taken clothes appropriate for the 'normal' Florida climate, in the form of tee-shirts, shorts, flip-flops and those other wardrobe items that simply cannot survive for more than thirty seconds in extreme winter conditions (and nor can the person wearing them), before they disintegrate. So, off we trotted to the shops to buy clothing for all of us that was more relevant.

When it was time for us to come back home, the bad weather had become very much badder, and was now the baddest it could be, with the whole area completely snowed in. The white stuff — lovely on a Christmas card, not so lovely in reality — and lots of it. And, what happens in places that are snowed in? That's right — no flights. Not a one, not in, nor out, and *definitely* no flights to the UK.

Eventually, we managed to get on a flight from Orlando to Tallahassee — that's the capital of Florida, for anyone swotting for a geography exam — then, from there a National Airlines flight to Frankfurt — that's in Germany, and it's the home of the appropriately named sausage. Please note: the later cessation of business for National Airlines had nothing to do with us flying on one of their planes.

As our plane approached its German destination, it was clear that the whole of Europe (and that's quite a big chunk of earth) was covered with what looked like a huge white tablecloth — more snow, and it was everywhere.

Something we wished *had been* covered, but perhaps not by snow, were the TV screens all around the terminal, which were showing — well, there's only one word to describe it, and that's *pornography*. And I mean really-not-good TV viewing, and certainly not what you want small children — or any size of children, for that matter — to observe.

We spent a frantic hour or so, trying desperately to keep the youngsters turned away from the screens, moving the poor things this way and that to avoid what was proving very difficult to avoid, and praying for some adverts to come on — although goodness knows what they might have been advertising!

Another 'eventually' passed by, miraculously without our offspring being mentally and emotionally scarred for life, then we were lucky enough to get a flight from Frankfurt to Manchester. Yippee! We were, of course, accompanied by an extra, brand-new, suitcase that we'd had to buy to carry all of the newly acquired winter apparel.

So much for our 'summer holiday' holiday.

***

In 1984, there was an endodontics meeting in Phoenix, Arizona, and, as this was at the time when I was finishing my MSc thesis, I decided to attend the meeting first and afterwards go on to Scottsdale, a pleasant town not far from Phoenix. I booked a rather nice hotel where I thought I could put the finishing touches to my tome, while relaxing by the pool and having my choice of delicious dishes from the hotel menu brought to me on request.

I knew that the Grand Canyon was in the vicinity, so before leaving Phoenix, I checked the map to see how far away it actually was — I'd never seen this incredible spectacle of nature before and it seemed like a good opportunity. My plan was simple — drive to the Canyon, enjoy the sights, drive back to Scottsdale, check in to the hotel and start work on finishing said thesis.

What is it they say about the best-laid plans of mice and men? And, what kind of things do mice plan, anyway? The drive, looking at the map, seemed to be about the same distance as going from Manchester to Birmingham (or Birmingham to Manchester, I'm guessing that would be the same).

So, conference well and truly over on the Saturday, on Sunday morning I hired a car, checked it had a full tank (of gas, not petrol, obviously) and set off on my lone quest to see the big hole in the ground.

With the town well behind me, fading into the dim and distant yonder, I drove the desert road. And I drove.

And I drove some more. I kept on driving, and then I realised the fuel gauge had been heading south, and at quite a pace. And still, I wasn't looking at the Grand Canyon, just more desert road. I know the Canyon is regarded as one of the seven wonders of the world, but I was just wondering if I'd ever get there.

The fuel tank in an American car was considerably smaller than its equivalent in a UK vehicle, hence you couldn't drive as far in the American car as you could in the UK car. I was familiar with this snippet of interesting and useful information, because I had owned an American car in the UK, and whenever I drove home to Manchester from London, I knew I had to switch off the air conditioning on the motorway at Warrington, otherwise I wouldn't make the rest of the journey without refuelling.

Anyway, there I was, still driving through the endless stretches of desert on either side, panicking now about ending up completely stranded, isolated from civilisation, in the middle of — well, a desert.

Although my situation was far from comical, it reminded me of those old Tom and Jerry cartoons where the 'scenery' was just a loop of a very basic picture — a cactus, a mountain, a rock, the same cactus, mountain, rock, and so on, endlessly.

Then, suddenly, like an oasis, there, just ahead, was a petrol station — I mean a gas station — and oh! the surge of relief that took over from the panic, fear and dread. It was overwhelming. I was saved, released from a short future of being baked alive by the scorching midday desert sun, my tongue so swollen from thirst I couldn't speak, feebly trying to fend off the giant lizards attacking my weakened body that they saw only as dinner... sorry, got a bit carried away there.

Filling a petrol (okay, gas) tank has never felt so good, so amazing, so totally life-changing — and I was so, so grateful. Tank full to bursting, I climbed back into the car and continued my journey, nerve-racking as it had been, to the Canyon.

Of course, because the drive had taken so long, I now didn't have time to enjoy the point of my desert trek *and* get back to Scottsdale, so I decided to take in the sights of the Grand Canyon then find a hotel somewhere in the area so I could spend the night, get some well-earned rest and make the return journey the next day. Sounds like a plan. Yes, another one.

From that day forward, I have always checked and double-checked the scale of any maps I've been looking at — especially in the US.

Manchester to Birmingham, my eye! — more like Manchester to Land's End.

***

Another of my Yankee Doodle wanderings was among my frequent trips to attend meetings of the American Association of Endodontists, of which Yours Truly was a member. Why wouldn't I be?

These meetings were usually held from a Wednesday through to the following Saturday, which suited me for two reasons: one, having a young family, I didn't want to leave my poor wife holding the baby (joke) on her own for too long, and two, because being Stateside for any longer would mean suffering jetlag when I was back home, which in turn meant I would be as much use to the family as a handbrake on a canoe and might as well have stayed in the US.

So, I would often leave home on a Wednesday morning and fly back to the UK on Saturday or Sunday night. And — this is the really clever bit — I would try to maintain my body clock on UK time. As smart as this was, I could only keep it up for three or four days, tops, but it did open up some interesting situations.

The Association's meetings were, like most events of this ilk, split into a morning session and an afternoon session, often starting off with a breakfast meeting. Later, after the morning session, we'd have a lunch meeting (otherwise known as 'lunch'). Get this for my cunning plan — if I had my breakfast at UK breakfast time, my lunch at UK lunchtime and my dinner at UK dinner time, then I could go straight to bed when the afternoon session ended. Clever, eh?

So, I ate my breakfast in the middle of the night (that's the middle of the night in the US, not the middle of the UK night — I hope you're following this), I had my lunch when they were having their breakfast (I don't think anyone ever suspected anything, mainly because I ate the same food they were eating, so only I knew what was going on), which would have been around twelve-thirty midday at home (I mean my UK home, not where I was staying over there), and I had dinner when they were having lunch, which would be around six p.m. in the UK. Then, as soon as afternoon lectures were finished, I popped off to my bed (that's my bed in the hotel in the States, not my bed at home in the UK).

Something I still remember clearly (not much falls into that category these days, quite honestly) is that I found an all-night diner — perfect for my requirements *vis-à-vis* keeping to the UK clock — near my hotel, making it even more perfect (when I say *my* hotel, I just mean the one I was staying at, I didn't own a hotel) and they served — wait for it — *Anytime Breakfast*. How amazing is that? It's as if they knew about my cunning plan. Spooky.

There I was, sitting at the bar — that's a food bar in a diner, not a drinks bar (these language issues can get quite complex), eating my breakfast one day (or it could have been one night — it's easy to lose track, isn't it, especially when you're eating something called *Anytime*?) and a big, burly police officer came in and sat next to me. I know, it does sound like the start of a joke, but don't worry, it isn't.

We got chatting, as you do in the middle of the night (or whenever) in a strange place (I mean I wasn't familiar with the place, I'm not being disparaging about it) in a far-off country halfway round the world, when you're eating food with a name that means it could be any time at all. He (my new-found pal, the policeman) was working a late shift and had popped in for his dinner.

I found it both odd and amusing that we were sitting together in the same place at the same time, but eating meals that should have been hours apart. Not only that, but I was eating breakfast, but not at breakfast time, and he was eating dinner, but not at dinnertime.

They say travel broadens the mind. Maybe they should say travel *baffles* the mind.

***

During the 1980s, I was working closely with a dentist in Chattanooga, Tennessee, USA (no, I don't mean physically close, I mean we collaborated from a distance — actually, over four thousand miles), and yes, that's the Chattanooga of *Choo-Choo* fame, courtesy of Glenn Miller, and Tennessee, the state famous for the country music of Nashville, the blues music of Memphis, and the Smokey Mountains that, as far as I can tell, have never produced any music, but — as always — I stand to be corrected.

This dentist invented — yes, I do mix with some really clever people — a new type of endodontic instrument, and Yours Truly acted as his agent in the UK for a while. On a trip to the States (one of many, as my Frequent Flyer miles will testify) I took a diversion to Chattanooga so that I could visit my dentist/inventor colleague in his practice, and we could catch up on business matters.

On my arrival at his surgery, I was surprised to see he was working with a microscope — something I'd never seen before in a dental practice, but it struck me as an interesting concept. The concept soon turned into reality and I purchased a microscope of my own to use in my practice.

I was due to arrive in Choo-Choo town on a Sunday, so my colleague kindly offered to meet me at the airport and I was invited to go out for dinner with him and his wife. He had booked a table at his country club and, after stopping off at my hotel, we would go on to his house to collect his wife, then all head for the country club, and our dinner. Easy, peasy.

Having just arrived after a lengthy flight lasting what seemed like weeks, my mode of dress was more 'relaxed for flying' than 'trussed up like a turkey for dinner' (the turkey being kosher, of course), so I needed to change into something more acceptable in the world of the country club. This caused a change of plan, and now my colleague suggested he should drop me at my hotel, then go home to pick up Mrs Colleague, then both of them would return to collect me (now suitably attired) and then we'd go off to the country club — and some dinner.

I unpacked and changed into something less comfortable, then my colleague arrived — but there was no wife. He was without wife, completely wifeless. So, we drove to his place, a mansion on Table Mountain, to collect the missing Mrs Colleague. I was starting to find Chattanooga rather complicated.

If I may intercept with a little geography lesson… Table Mountain is not really a mountain, but more of a hill (in UK terms, anyway, but the Americans do tend to exaggerate) and it looks out over a valley, on the other side of which lies the city of Atlanta. Atlanta is the home of that world-famous fizzy drink, Coca-Cola.

Interesting fact — Coca-Cola was first sold in Atlanta in 1886 by a Dr John Pemberton, and one of the ingredients of this tasty beverage was cocaine, hence the 'Coca' part of the name. Around 1903, this was removed from the recipe and the resulting liquid was sold to young people known as 'soda jerks', who worked in drug stores, operating the then-popular soda fountain to produce drinks from flavoured syrups and carbonated water. You learn something every day.

Because this Coca-Cola was a new product with no track record, in order to persuade these soda jerks to buy the Coca-Cola concentrate, they were offered shares in the new Coca-Cola company. It was, if you like, a perk. A jerk perk. Some accepted this offer, and went on to buy up those shares not taken up by other less adventurous jerks, thereby building up a shareholding in what became a multi-billion-dollar company.

As we drove up the hill (apologies to our American friends — I mean mountain), my colleague pointed out certain houses, all massive mansions, telling me this one is now the home of the grandson of one of the original jerks, that one belongs to the grandson of the guy who first bottled the drink in its infancy, the next impressive abode is owned by the grandson of the chap who invented the vending machine that later sold the bottles of Coca-Cola. It was rather annoying to see these fabulous places, bought with cash from the sales of a sugary drink that destroys teeth, when my work is to help people keep their teeth healthy. Difficult not to feel a bit miffed.

Having had this verbal illustration of the type of people inhabiting this local area, I assumed that perhaps these people would be members of the country club, this select institution sitting atop the hill that was pretending to be a mountain.

Anyway, we arrived at Dr and Mrs Colleague's magnificent home and Mrs Colleague was duly collected, then we really did drive to the country club this time — and I was by now really looking forward to my dinner. After all that faffing about, we arrived and were met by the valet (posh bouncer), who welcomed us with all the warmth of a nineteenth-century polar expedition.

Valet: *Good evening, Dr Smith, Mrs Smith.*

Dr Colleague replied: *Good evening, this is Dr Cohen from Manchester, England.*

Valet: *Good evening, Dr Cohen, welcome to our country club.*

Once inside, we were met and greeted (yes, twice within minutes) by the *maître d'*, who repeated the valet's welcome.

Maître d': *Good evening, Dr Smith, Mrs Smith.*

Dr Colleague replied: *Good evening, this is Dr Cohen from Manchester, England.*

Maître d': *Good evening, Dr Cohen.*

Then he said something different, which really threw me after the monotony of all the 'good evening' repetition.

Maître d': *Dr Smith, would you like to have cocktails at the bar, or would you prefer to go straight to your table?*

Dr Colleague answered for all of us, seeing as it was *his* country club, not mine, or even Mrs Colleague's, that we would go to the table, for which I was incredibly grateful, since I was now *so* hungry, I could eat the proverbial scabby horse. I didn't say it out loud because I had no idea what the locals would make of translating that.

Our table had the most stunning view (through a window, of course — we weren't sitting outdoors) across the valley, with the Atlanta skyline illuminated against the evening sky over on the other side.

Dr Colleague ordered champagne (well, what did you expect?) and — shock, horror! — this fancy schmancy country club *didn't have any champagne chilled!* Good grief! What is the world coming to? The *maître d'* swiftly apologised, bending almost double in his affected humility, and offered to quickly chill some if we could give him 'a few minutes'. Dr Colleague told him that would be fine.

Now, here's a revelation. I don't like champagne, I'm more of a spirits man, myself. Can't see the point of wine. White wine tastes like flavoured lemonade and red gives me a headache.

The required few minutes passed by and the *maître d'* returned, carrying a suitably chilled bottle, perfectly clothed in a starched, brilliant white napkin. He held the bottle correctly, with his thumb in the hollow of the glass base, and poured it perfectly. But, as he was pouring, I noticed the label. It wasn't champagne — it was Spanish Freixenet Cava, Black Label, which we used to pay less than a tenner for in Spain.

I never saw the bill for the evening, but I bet anything you like that Dr Colleague was charged a whole lot more than that.

***

I believe I've mentioned previously my number one rule in life, i.e., SK *(Sport Kills)*. A jogger I am not, nor do I pay an eye-watering monthly membership to frequent a crowded, sweaty gym to make myself feel good (and kid myself I look good). I have no desire to show off a new lycra ensemble that cost an arm and a leg, the likes of which can only ever look anywhere close to acceptable on a physically perfect specimen of humanity.

In addition to my aversion to sport, there are two other aspects of life that I am not happy with. One is getting up with the lark, at the crack of sparrows, as I'm more of a night owl than an early bird. The other thing is that I'm not really comfortable around animals. I know (even if I don't understand) that most people seem to want to share their existence with a dog, a cat, a budgie, or any other creature they regard as a pet these days (a friend of ours even has a large — i.e., *long* — snake), but Yours Truly, however, does not. This lack of desire for a herd of Friesians in my home or garden applies mainly to one species — the dog. And please don't ask me why, as I have no idea.

Sometime in the 1980s, I was invited to give a lecture to the students and faculty of a dental school in Hertford, Connecticut. The invitation came from a Norwegian Professor and Doctor of Dental Surgery, who — I found out some time later — was a true hero in the Second World War, as a member of the Norwegian Underground Army, while Norway was occupied by Nazi Germany from 1940 to 1945. His efforts helped in the liberation of his country and he was awarded the Norwegian War Medal with Star in 1945.

If I had known what an amazing man the professor was *before* I accepted his kind invitation to stay at his lovely family home the night before the lecture, I would have been so in awe of him, it wouldn't have mattered that the price I had to pay for the overnight accommodation was having no choice but to get up early and then go for a walk with him — and his dog!

I am honoured to have met Dr Langeland — even though it meant spending time with his four-legged friend!

***

The US organisation that held the dental convention in Florida (the memorable visit enhanced by a monsoon) choose a different location each year for the convention, and one year they decided to hold it in Phoenix, Arizona.

Even though the timing of this event was always between Christmas and New Year, Arizona's weather is pretty good all year round, apart from the summers, when it gets *really hot*. So hot that many locals depart for the mountains (we really would call them hills) where it's much cooler.

My wife and I decided to go to the Phoenix convention and were hoping to catch a bit of winter sun in the Arizona desert — while I would be learning and networking, of course.

The chosen venue was a 'resort hotel'. In the States, this normally means that the hotel is spread over extensive grounds and often the bedrooms are chalets around the outside of the main building. That's exactly how this place turned out to be. Unfortunately, the weather didn't follow suit and was not at all as we'd expected — in fact, it was pretty awful.

Of course, we had learned precisely nothing from our previous climate-thwarted trips, and had landed there with only summer clothes in our luggage. Not a fleece or a balaclava between us.

By the second day, it was so cold we almost froze getting from our chalet to the main hotel, and we were only driven to venture outside by the fact that everything we needed was in this main section — including food, which we would obviously need at some point, frozen or not.

However, to save us from impending hypothermia, there was a shop in the hotel foyer and — lo and behold! — they were selling fleeces. Hurrah! Sadly, they all had the resort's logo emblazoned in prominent display across the front. I retract my 'Hurrah!'

We now possess a set of winter clothes purchased under pressure, to add to those purchased under the stress of possible drowning in Florida.

Need I say that, in future, wherever we are heading around the globe (and possibly elsewhere?) we have agreed to take a selection of outfits to cover every weather eventuality.

My wife calls these our 'Justin clothes' — just in case!

***

It didn't take long after The Big Fire of 2001 (I mentioned this in my Los Angeles saga) for us to realise (because we're so sharp and nothing gets past us) that we needed brand new equipment for all of the surgeries, once the new premises were found. Be patient, you will learn all about this fire in the 'Fanning the Flames' chapter, coming up soon.

With endodontics being so big in the US, the American professional journals were constantly advertising equipment suitable for endodontic practices, so I decided to design my new surgery around the American model (no, not Jerry Hall). In order to achieve this, I needed to buy some specialist hardware from a company based in Denver, Colorado. The equipment was all modular so there were a number of combinations available.

So, another trip to the States to add to my collection! I don't remember exactly when I went, but it was sometime between the practice going up in smoke and the point when we moved into the new premises (just realised how obvious that is).

Denver is known as the Mile High City (as opposed to the Mile High Club, which is a totally different matter altogether, and something of which I know absolutely nothing) and the Town Hall steps have a marker on one step indicating the exact location of one mile above sea level. I did have a bit of a problem with the altitude and rarefied atmosphere (that's lack of oxygen to those who don't watch David Attenborough documentaries) in the form of nose bleeds.

As I was staying here for about four days in total, I thought why not hire an aircraft and have a bit of a fly around (because I have a private pilot's licence so I can do that), as I fancied seeing the high mountains and very famous ski resorts in the area.

I had to fly with a co-pilot, a chap who was an instructor at the local airfield where I rented the plane (because when you have a UK pilot's licence in the US, you have to do that). I found out that there are different ways of setting up an aircraft at altitude — something I wasn't familiar with, since most of my flying was in Europe, therefore quite low and close to sea level.

We took off from the airfield and passed over the mountains and ski resorts — all quite magnificent when viewed from the air (or should I say, viewed from the plane up in the air: we weren't just hanging in the air — that would be weird). Anyway, there I was, enjoying my flight and the lovely sights below, when suddenly — all of the electrical instruments in the aircraft stopped working, all at the same time. One second, they were working and the next — gone, dead, expired. Gulp.

I must explain that an aircraft engine doesn't work like a car engine (not that most of us know much about how our cars function, and that's why mechanics are in business). No, the aircraft engine has dynamos that create electrical energy (using electro-magnetism, but let's not get technical) which means it can keep the engine running. What it *can't* do is produce sufficient of this energy to keep some of the instrumentation working. That, unfortunately, included the electronic navigation system (satnav to us mere mortals) and the communications equipment, the bit that keeps the plane in contact with Air Traffic Control. So, nothing to worry about. Much.

The instructor, to my great relief, assured me that this situation wasn't a problem, given that he knew the area very well (believe me when I say his expertise in local geography did nothing to quell my angst), but he did say we should head back to the airfield as soon as possible. Sooner would have suited me. While I did the flying bit (because I can) he played around with — sorry, I mean, he made some technical adjustments to the on-board equipment, which led him to diagnose a problem with the alternator.

Just as we were approaching the airfield, he managed to get the electrics up and running again, which meant we could then inform Air Traffic Control of our death-defying time in the skies above the skis. Scary stuff, but once again Yours Truly lived to tell the tale, so I have.

This nerve-racking, breath-holding, pulse-quickening episode didn't manage to put me off flying, fortunately.

Some years later, when our dental practice was in the hands of a corporate outfit, it was decided to hold a competition to find our biggest referrers (that's the people who recommended patients to us) and when I say the biggest ones, that means those who referred the most patients, not the fattest ones. Because my periodontist partner was a massive football fan (again, not fat, just a big fan), unlike my good self — SK *(Sport Kills)*, remember? — the prize being dangled in front of those taking part was box tickets.

I have no idea what that means, but I am reliably informed thus: you get to watch the football match from the comfort of an enclosed area with proper seats and tables, where you can have food and drinks served and sit in the warm and dry while the *hoi polloi* are outside, crammed on hard wooden benches, exposed to the elements and unable to choose who they sit next to.

The box tickets were for a Manchester United game, and for those who, like me, don't follow sports, Man U, as they are commonly known, is a team of football players representing Manchester. If you are reading this in the USA (you never know — this might go global) that's a soccer team.

So, to avoid anything and everything to do with this, I offered my own prize for the two top winners, and that was — drum roll, please — lunch with me in France, flown there and back in my plane. And yes, with me doing the flying. The two lucky winners were a lady from Wales and a chap from Manchester. Believe it or not, he turned down this amazing opportunity, but asked if his associate could take his place, to which I agreed, being the nice person I am.

The three of us flew down to Le Touquet in the most amazingly clear weather, and enjoyed a fantastic lunch in the highly acclaimed restaurant there, which is actually sited on the airfield tarmac. After the meal, a quick tour of the south coast before heading home, when suddenly (no, not the electrics this time) the weather took a turn. It wasn't a turn for the better.

Thank goodness, the associate (who really wasn't even meant to be there) turned out to be an instinctive navigator and a great map reader, both of which went a long way in getting us back safely.

Due to this unwanted bad weather, we had to take a different route and the lady from Wales had to be taken back to Manchester, instead of where she wanted to be — Wales. Once landed and thankfully back on *terra firma*, I took her by car to Liverpool, where her husband met us.

After all that, would you believe it — I got a speeding ticket.

Part-Time Plumber

Many years ago, in a bygone age, when our children were still quite young…

Actually, they still seem very young to us, but I suppose that's because, as they have aged, so have we and the gap between us, therefore, remains constant (there must be someone, perhaps in the world of Einstein's theory of relativity, who could explain it better, but for now I'm all you've got).

My granddaughter, sweet little child that she is, has a wonderful way of explaining the different age groups of those around her. We, the grandparents and elders of the family, are *olderlies*; our children, including her own parents, are *middlies*; and she and her peers are *youngerlies*. These terms remain in use, despite my wife's constant attempts (with some bribery involved, I have no doubt) to affect a reclassification of the groups, wherein the *olderlies* would be amalgamated with the *middlies,* thereby making us *olderlies* feel much better about it.

All such attempts at negotiation have met with a brick wall, in the form of a small child, unmoving, unspeaking and wide-eyed, standing with hands on hips (the most defiant stance of the very young), her whole manner telling anyone in her immediate vicinity, and possibly some further afield, not to bother trying to persuade, cajole or argue, because it ain't happening.

Where was I? Oh, yes — when the children were still young, we decided to take a family holiday with two other families, both couples being good friends of ours. We chose a 'family friendly' hotel on the south coast, hoping and praying that the description covered 'child-proof' and would therefore mean the place had a chance of remaining standing after our stay, and whatever associated punishment the mob of kids would vent on the place, or, indeed, on the whole of the Bournemouth region.

Among the attractions and facilities the place had to offer, swimming pool box ticked, was a 'night listening service' — something that would have parents of today running screaming for the hills. Their screaming would no doubt include the words 'abuse', 'invasion', 'privacy', 'rights' and many others of similar tone.

However, this was then, and the night listening service meant that we (adults, slash parents) could feed them (children) their tea 'early' then we (still the adults but with the parenting being less hands-on) could enjoy a leisurely dinner together, completely sprog-less.

In our group, the three fathers all had professional careers, with Yours Truly a dentist, one friend a doctor and the other a solicitor. There is a problem when holidaying if you are going to let this knowledge seep out, and that is — the Freebie Consultation.

As soon as people find out you are a professional in an area in which they would normally approach you as a client/patient, they immediately behave as though you were in your office/surgery and start asking for advice, opinions, even a diagnosis and costs — and some go further and cannot help themselves asking you *Could you just have a look at this?* or *Can you feel this lump here — what d'you think it is*? as they expose an area of their physicality not normally viewed by the pool at a hotel in Bournemouth, or thrust their face into yours, with their mouth wide open. Seriously, it doesn't add to the holiday feelgood factor for us.

So, before we embarked on this holiday, we agreed to leave our 'proper jobs' at home, and adopt something less open to such invasion by one and all. My friends became a joiner and an electrician, while Yours Truly chose to wear the hat of a plumber (do plumbers wear hats? I never noticed). This was quite fitting for me, as I've always thought of my work in dentistry as 'oral plumbing'.

Once ensconced in the hotel, unpacked and with many deep breaths being drawn, we met a family from Scotland. In a matter of minutes, our children had begun playing with their children and the entire brood of the four families made it clear they would like to spend their holiday together — because, let's face it, the kids are in charge.

We were by the pool one day when the father of the Scottish family suddenly got into trouble in the deep end and was obviously struggling. My doctor pal and I dived in (well, he dived in and in my case it was really jumping in — to this day, I've never been able to dive) and got the poor chap to the edge of the pool and then out of the water.

He was fine, and very grateful for our assistance, and we spent some time chatting with him. It turned out he was an accountant — ah! the complete set, like in the card game 'Happy Families'. It almost sounds like the beginning of a joke — one day, a doctor, a dentist, a solicitor and an accountant were chatting…

Anyway, we explained to him our clever ruse of pretending to be the joiner, the electrician and the plumber, and told him he should join us so that he, too, could avoid the inevitable *What tax d'you think I should be paying on that?* and so on. We appointed him a painter and decorator.

In the times of which I speak, every holiday hotel of this type had a special feature. This came in the form of a resident grandmother, that older lady who always sat in the same chair in the same place in the lounge every evening, and woe betide anyone who attempted a *coup* on that chair. As soon as you first clapped eyes on her, you knew this was the ritual and you had to obey. Or else. And this lady, from her constant viewpoint, was a people watcher, and subsequently she would soon glean everything there was to know — about everybody in the place.

One particular evening, when all of our four-family group were standing around together, casually chatting and relaxed, from her throne in the lounge, this lady summoned us over to her floral-curtained court. I say 'summoned' but she actually *ordered* us over. And, like schoolboys to the Head's office, we went.

After looking each of us up and down, slowly and deliberately, with an icy glare that could freeze an erupting volcano, she declared, *I don't believe for one second that you four men are a joiner, an electrician, a plumber and a decorator. And what's more* — at this point, she raised her hand and, pointing a finger at each of us in turn, added, *you're a lawyer* (she obviously thought our legal pal deserved a promotion), *you're a doctor, you're a dentist and you are an accountant.*

The scary thing is, she was dead right every time. How she knew is still a mystery to this day. The wisdom of age? Or maybe Einstein told her.

Men in White Coats

Although the mid-1970s saw an explosion in the world of fashion, influenced by not only the hippie and other eclectic styles of the previous decade, but copying some styles from the 1940s and '50s as well, this mammoth shift in the contents of the British wardrobe did not filter through to the work attire of the humble dentist.

The much-coveted clinical scrubs were not for the lowly dental practice, being reserved for the higher echelons of hospital operating theatres. No, in those days, we mere mortals turned up at work, took off our outer garments and donned a plain, simple, button-through white coat over our shirt and trousers. No frills, no fuss. Had it not been for the chair and the drill, we could have been mistaken for the ice cream man.

I was well aware that my wife did not include ironing in her list of favourite pastimes, not by any stretch, so I decided I would be on my way to the *Husband of the Year* award if I could find a version of the white coat that didn't need to be pressed but would still look the part. This innovative garment would simply go into the washer, be removed and popped on a coat hanger until completely dry. Easy, peasy, as they say.

The only type I could find at the time was made of nylon, which definitely did not need ironing — indeed, any such application of heat would have reduced the entire coat to a fizzing blob stuck to the bottom of the iron.

So, I bought a supply of these incredibly practical (not to mention useful in the award-winning stakes) nylon coats, wore them each day at work and took them home to be washed when required.

And so, life went on. Until...

I was working in those days in a practice located in an area where a large proportion of the local population followed a certain religion which demanded the married women to wear wigs whenever they ventured outside into the community. Many of these ladies were, of course, patients at the practice.

One such lady was lying back on the treatment couch, with her head close to my chest as I leaned over her to begin my work. Then, to my utter horror, her head began to move closer and closer, as if detaching itself from her body.

For a nanosecond, or even less time than that, I actually thought her head was falling off — it was the fright of my life, believe me.

It turned out that she had chosen to buy a nylon wig, which was much less costly than the natural hair models on the market, and my nylon coat getting close to this caused a static charge that was obviously sufficient to draw the wig off the lady's head and on to my chest.

I know some people think a visit to the dentist can be a hair-raising experience, but... seriously? Come on!

Dear Margot

They say money is the root of all evil. Meandering along a canal on a beautifully decorated narrowboat is a most pleasurable experience.

So, we can use the word 'root' and the word 'canal' without anybody batting an eyelid. But you put them together and everyone runs screaming for the hills.

Root canal. A phrase to drive terror into the hearts of even the most intrepid and fearless of individuals. In the 1980s it was common practice for me and my colleagues to carry out root canal treatments in two separate sessions, and, as professional literature on the subject was, to say the least, minimal, we had no reason to suspect that what we were doing was anything but correct.

A lady came in for treatment one day — we can call her Margot (that's not her name, but I have no desire to venture into litigious waters, if it's all the same to you) — and I explained to her about the work being completed over two appointments. She replied (as if I hadn't spoken a single word) that we must do all of the work in just one go. Just like that, the patient *told us* how it had to be!

Margot, who was about my age, was, shall we say, a somewhat persuasive lady, clearly someone who was used to getting her own way. My mind ran away with itself briefly and I had a momentary vision of a little worried-looking man in a kitchen, scurrying around, preparing dinner, wearing a pinny and Marigolds and desperately hoping that the missus was *not* having a bad time at the dentist. I felt for my imaginary friend, the poor battered husband.

I'm sorry, but my professional (I emphasised the word 'professional' and leaned forward at the same time, giving her the most dominant eye contact I could muster) *advice is that you have this work done over two separate appointments, because I cannot guarantee one hundred per cent the efficacy of such treatment, should it not be done in this manner.*

Pulling myself up to my full five feet and eight inches, I drew a breath and said, *I really do have to insist on this.*

Margot didn't even blink. She just lowered her eyelids to half-mast and said, slowly and calmly, *No, I am telling you, you will do all of the work in one session.*

Huh! So much for my efforts in word emphasis, body language and eye contact! It was almost as if she were my senior professional and I were the trainee.

Okay, I sighed (audibly, so she would know I wasn't happy with her), *I'm prepared to do this — but with one condition.*

I allowed a couple of seconds to pass, for dramatic effect, and did the leaning-forward thing again.

Should you experience any problems — and I mean any at all — following this treatment, I can accept no responsibility whatsoever. I will also have to note this conversation in full on your patient file.

What sort of problems?

I detected, at last, some interest. Most people would be feeling a bit concerned at the prospect of 'any problems' after such treatment, but not our Margot. Still with eyes at half-mast, she listened as I reeled off the potential issues that we (the actual professionals) knew could possibly happen. It's quite a list.

That did it, apparently.

When I finished speaking, Margot's eyelids re-elevated and, without any apology or acceptance that I had been right all along, of course, she agreed to attend for the *two* visits for treatment.

Not long after Margot's memorable attendance at the surgery, my professor at the dental school asked me if I would carry out a literature review regarding any evidence as to whether single-visit treatment or multiple-visit treatment had any benefits over the other.

It pains me to admit it, but I could find not a scrap of proof to show that the two-visit system was any better.

What pains me even more (and quite honestly, I'm

having a bit of a problem putting this into words), is to accept that — whether she actually knew it or not — Margot could have been right.

My (Bad) Dream Car

James Bond, 007. Likes his martinis shaken, not stirred. Likes his women stunning. And dangerous. And he drives some fabulous cars. Yes, I know it's only in films, but I was a young man, and young men can dream. Can, do, and always will.

The car that came to be associated with this enigma that was Agent 007, as portrayed by the inimitable Sean Connery, was the Aston Martin, and as soon as I saw Connery's invincible character behind the wheel, escaping from his latest death-defying confrontation with some evil billionaire megalomaniac who lived inside a mountain amid disgustingly extravagant luxury, with a big fat furry cat (who looked equally evil) and a bevvy of jaw-droppingly beautiful women, all trained to kill with a single exquisitely manicured fingernail, who waited on him hand and foot, providing for his every vile whim… well, I wanted one.

Aston Martin by Freddie, aged 8

And this hero was more than invincible. He was intellectual, suave, cool, stylish, manly, handsome, brave, sexy… all of those words that describe how every young man wants (and hopes, even if he only has faint hope) to be regarded.

I'm just starting to wonder if all of this hero-takes-on-the-world imagery and cheating death on a daily basis might have had something to do with my intense *amour* for the car. Anyway, whatever the basis for my desire, I really, *really* did want an Aston Martin.

Being dad to three kids who were all being privately educated, as well as studying for my MSc and PhD, meant that my disposable income didn't quite put me in the position of being a potential buyer of said dream machine. But I never gave up hope.

In time, with the offspring now grown and me well established in my specialist practice, I eventually arrived at a time in my life when the possibility of actually owning an (albeit second-hand) Aston Martin even more actually became a reality. Then, it occurred to me that I had never even been in one.

So, when I found I had in my chair a patient who, I knew, drove an Aston Martin, I seized an opportunity to correct this. He actually owned not one, but two, Astons (how dare he, when Yours Truly didn't even have one?) — a DB7 and a DB9.

He had driven to the surgery on this day in the DB7 (so nice for him to have a choice), which, oddly, he was about to off-load. Oh, joy! When I'd finished his treatment, I had some free time so I asked him if he could take me for a spin in the car, seeing as I was definitely interested. He could, and off we went.

On returning to the practice, once I had managed to extricate myself, body and all four limbs, (preferably still joined together) from the car, my back — an area of my physical being that had never really been good — was in such a state that the matter was decided for me. There was no way I could subject myself to such torture, not even in the imagined guise of 007.

So, after all the years of wishing and hoping, and then finally being this close to realising my dream — shattering disappointment.

But hey! That's life.

Fifteen Minutes of Fame

While I was studying for my MSc, my main supervisor (as I have mentioned earlier) was a very highly qualified organic chemist (it was the chemistry that was organic, not the chap — there again, being a human...) who specialised in dental materials.

He always told me, *the hardest part of getting a PhD is actually being selected for admission*, which prompts a mental image of a massive crowd, all clamouring to be selected, with me in the middle, jumping up and down and shouting, *Pick me! Pick me!* (I never did that, honestly.)

Further down that road, when I received my MSc, I told Marsha — and anyone else who might have been prepared to listen — that this was now the end of my studying, no more life as any kind of student, absolutely not, and I was going to get back into work to provide properly for my family. These were approximately the same words, give or take, that I had uttered when I received my original degree at the end of my time at university. So, it was now 1984, I had my MSc, and I did return to full-time work.

Two years later, my MSc supervisor as was, and Manchester University, *invited me* to undertake some research, leading to a PhD. Given his words of wisdom regarding selection, how could I possibly refuse?

It was during this research — and totally by accident — that I discovered something that could possibly become a new material for use in dentistry. Me... Yours Truly... discovering something amazing! I was really, really excited about this and the University was also excited (I'm not talking about the building, I mean the people who ran it). So much so, they applied for a number of patents on the material and on the method of manufacture.

Of course, I'd never applied for a patent before — my father had, some years ago, but not for a dental material (that would be a really weird coincidence) — so, under the guidance of those who knew about such things (always a good idea to be led by people who know stuff when you don't) we (that's my supervisor and me) set about preparing a document in which I (we) had to detail every last little thing about the material and also every last little thing about the mode of manufacturing said material. That's a lot of things, even if they are little.

Once finished, the document would go off (well, it wouldn't just *go* under its own steam — I had to send it, obviously) to a specialist Patent Agent, whose job was to translate my (our) collection of information into the language used in the world of patents — 'patentese', if you like. Then, that information, duly regurgitated, would be sent to the relevant patent offices, in this case both the UK and US.

Once again, Yours Truly goes international!

A few weeks after sending the application off, a large package arrived, containing a thick wad of papers, with a covering letter asking that the contents be checked before submission. This document was, by now, so different from the original notes I'd (we'd) prepared that it wasn't clear if it was actually my (our) patent application, or perhaps someone else's that had been sent to me (us) in error. I (we) did check with the agent but he confirmed that it really was mine (ours), so that will give you an idea of the likelihood of me (us) checking through it all with any hope of confirming its accuracy — or not, as the case may be.

The result of all this confusion was that three separate patents were, in fact, granted, so one can only assume that the patents offices and the patent agent both spoke the same version of 'patentese'.

What happened after this came as a bit of a shock. Firstly, the local evening newspaper, the *Manchester Evening News*, got hold of the 'story' and published an article about my 'novel invention' and its unusual heritage! I honestly don't remember if they contacted anyone to get some background information, but the article appeared anyway.

After this, as if a domino effect had been activated by some higher force, the local BBC radio station also picked up on the 'story' and they did contact me for more detail and background to the 'invention'. This led to Yours Truly being interviewed on Radio Manchester's breakfast show. Fame at last.

The only problem with appearing (in a sound-only way, of course, because it's radio) in a 'breakfast' show, as opposed to an 'afternoon' or 'evening' show, is that you have to get up really early — I've made my thoughts on this very clear, so you know I'm not a fan.

But who could resist enjoying their 'Fifteen Minutes of Fame'? Most definitely not me.

Group Lobotomy?

1991. The year I obtained my PhD. Hurrah! It was also the year when I let myself be persuaded to do some teaching.

I would spend two half-days a week at the clinic in the local dental hospital, imparting my wisdom, if not my wisdom teeth, to a group of undergraduate dental students.

To begin with, I would teach general procedures, the likes of amalgam fillings, white adhesive fillings, and very, very occasionally, root fillings — which was a shame because that was my speciality. This fact, for some reason, evaded those in charge, the Higher Beings, so it was a bit like being in the army where, if your skills lay in the catering world, you'd be given a tank to drive, and if you were talented in woodwork, you'd be appointed chief cook.

Gradually, the light bulb came on and it dawned on the students, and then on my fellow faculty members, that root fillings were my *forté*, my *pièce de résistance*, my *métier*... although you'd be forgiven for thinking it might be French vocabulary.

And so, it came to pass, and I ended up teaching mostly root filling procedures. Happy me.

But, there's always a 'but', and this one was that some of the students, in my humble opinion, should never have been selected to take up such a manually dextrous profession as dentistry. Not in a month of Sundays. Don't get me wrong, they were all really bright academics, because you needed at least two As and a B at A-level to get into dental school. They were nice kids, too.

But (yes, another one), in spite of my pearls of wisdom being cast before them, their ability in the area of dental plumbing was not their strong suit. Far from. Very, very far.

Casualties were many and frequent, with cut lips and tongues being stitched, following what we described to the patients as 'a little local problem'. I could only assume they put up with this collateral damage because their treatment was free.

This problem had to be rationalised.

How could such academically gifted students do these things? I pondered awhile. Then it came to me. The students had lectures from nine until ten o'clock each morning, and between four and five o'clock each afternoon; in between, they treated (or mistreated) the patients at the clinic. I assume they also had lunch at some point.

So, I came up with a scenario to explain what was happening. With morning lectures over, the students would go down to the basement, open their lockers and change into the appropriate clinical wear. Actually, that's a bit of an overstatement, since 'clinical wear' back then was, as mentioned previously, a simple button-through white coat worn over whatever day clothes the students had dragged on that morning. The twenty-first century Health and Safety Police would have a field day, but the only policing that took place was in the form of my colleague, John, reprimanding the male students for the absence of a tie, and a lady named Hilary, equally my colleague, reprimanding the females for skirt hemlines a little on the high side.

Anyway, white coats donned, and as perfectly co-ordinated as a ballroom dance team, the students would raise their hands slowly to their heads and, like a scene from the worst horror movie ever, their fingers would push into their skulls, lifting out their brains, and placing them carefully in the lockers. Then, without any trace of the *Shaun of the Dead* brain removal, they would report to the clinic.

Come four o'clock, this procedure would be acted out in reverse and they would trot off to their afternoon lectures.

With the ham-fisted dentistry performed by the students on such a regular basis, and the ensuing apology-strewn repairs to many patients, this weird horror fantasy is what got me through those days.

***

Some years later, I had occasion to repeat this horrific analogy when I was appointed to the dizzy heights of Chairman of a local management committee.

The other members — academics, successful entrepreneurs, business professionals and so on — all possessed far greater intellect than I, and yet some of the rubbish they came out with was — well, it was just that. Rubbish.

And so, to get me through the committee proceedings and get-togethers with these drivel-spouting intellectuals, I would imagine them walking through the door, removing their brains and placing them carefully on the table, then taking their seats for the meeting.

More drivel spouted and meeting ended, they would gather round the table, replace their brains and be on their merry way.

As mad as it sounds, this at least prevented me from losing my temper, starting a shouting match, storming out, or several other options that should not be spoken of in this particular tome.

The Boy Band Next Door

It was the mid-to-late 1990s, and our practice was housed in a Georgian building in an area that was being largely redeveloped, just south of Manchester city centre.

It was rapidly becoming a highly desirable locale.

Next door was an old warehouse, one of those solidly built structures that hawk-eyed property developers describe as 'ripe for conversion', even though their plans have nothing to do with religion, and their selling prices cannot be described as Christian generosity. And so, this big building was now a collection of futuristic goldfish-bowl office suites and, on the upper floors, a small number of des-res apartments, homes for those who presumably hate gardening and enjoy travelling in lifts.

One of the goldfish bowl offices — sorry, twentieth-century workspaces — was occupied by our local independent radio station, Key 103.

Inhabiting one of the overpriced bedsits — oops! my mistake, I mean luxury apartments — was a member of a very popular boy band who had emerged, with their baggy jeans and baby faces, from obscurity in the local area into the dazzling world of pop stars.

This band enjoyed the adoration of a whole generation of young female fans, who apparently made it their sole purpose in life to try to get close to these band members, and — something I never worked out and was constantly puzzled by — they always seemed to know whenever this particular young chap was in residence and when he wasn't.

How they gleaned this information was a source of much wonder and bemusement to me. Had they all chipped in their pocket money to hire a private investigator to follow the poor lad wherever he went? Or maybe they had access to some 007-type technology that beeped when he came within a mile of his new home? I was fascinated.

In the early days, when he'd first moved in, these girls would suddenly appear, like a swarm of giggling locusts, and they would attempt to enter the building. Actually, it was more like *storming* the building, there were so many of them and they were all jumping about, shouting, squealing and chattering in some sort of frenzy — honestly, it was quite scary.

But the building had excellent security (another excuse to hike up the price of each unit) and so the gaggle of giggling girl fans never made it through the highly polished entry doors. (I avoided looking at the place on sunny days — the reflection could probably burn your retinas.)

Having been given their marching orders by the security guards, these determined devotees put Plan B into operation, which was to congregate in our car park and wait for a glimpse of their heart's desire. I have no idea where their parents thought they were, but these youngsters seemed to be inhabiting our car park at all hours of the day and night.

We would arrive for work in the morning to find the place littered with empty Coca-Cola cans — apparently the staple diet of these pop fans, and a sign of just how young they were, as they weren't drinking any alcohol. We tried everything we could think of to stop them using our area for their stalking activities (we did stop short of employing any strong-arm tactics as demonstrated by next-door's newly installed and possibly a little over-zealous security) but nothing deterred them.

One day, our new neighbour turned up at the practice, asking if we could offer him dental treatment. He was dressed in the regulation boy-band uniform — scruffy jeans, un-ironed t-shirt, and ridiculously expensive designer trainers, the latter being the result of an inordinate amount of technological research (if you believe the TV ads).

The young man was allocated to one of my colleagues, a general dentist who was by now in his senior years. After a thorough examination of this very famous mouth, he came up with a rather costly treatment plan and his new patient trotted off to Reception to arrange the various appointments to accommodate the work required. The dentist, who clearly knew even less than I did about boy bands, came to speak to the rest of us, and he appeared rather concerned.

Can this guy actually afford my fees, d'you think?

With much hilarity, we assured him that, not only could the young chap pay any bill we presented to him, but he could probably buy us all out several times over!

A Language of Our Own

In the world of dentistry, as I've mentioned before, my specific line of work is root canal treatment, known in the profession as endodontics. I can almost hear you groaning.

One of the things we do in this particular aspect of dental work is to place a rubber sheet over the mouth — and, since the Covid-19 pandemic took over our lives — over the nose as well.

This cover is called a rubber dam. We cut a hole in the sheet to expose the tooth requiring our attention and the sheet is held in place by a frame made of either plastic or metal, and the plan necessitating all of this palaver is to prevent any saliva (that's posh for dribble or spit), which is infected, contaminating the tooth which by now has been disinfected. Plus (because we always give value for money) it also stops the disinfectant, which is slightly toxic (otherwise it wouldn't be capable of disinfecting anything) going into the patient's mouth and down their throat.

I know some people wonder why the disinfectant can't be better tasting, and I say to them, *If it tastes good, it's not disinfectant.*

If it's not disinfectant, it's not protecting your tooth from being infected. If your tooth does get infected during the procedure, then not only is my work here not done, but you could possibly sue me as well. So, the rubber dam protects us both in very different ways.

Still demonstrating the multi-functionality of the rubber dam, it helps the patient to keep their mouth open (very useful for me, please note) during what is a rather lengthy procedure.

And, there's more. It *psychologically separates* the patient from the tooth, so it can almost seem that the tooth is external to the patient's mouth and so the drilling, filling, and anything else ending in 'ing', is not happening to the patient, but only to the tooth.

And finally, and in some cases most importantly, it prevents the patient from talking. Or, should I say, they may attempt some conversation but I won't understand a word that comes out of their (very wide open) mouth. Strangely, at the time of writing *vis-à-vis* the Covid-19 pandemic, with my own protective mask, making me look like I'm about to audition for the part of Darth Vader, they can't make out anything I say, either.

So, this weird and wonderful scenario results in some strange (and totally incomprehensible) conversations...

Me:	*Ehrrff ooh meemohn allnay?*
	Trans: Have you been on holiday?
Patient:	*Nnnggghhhaaa*
	Trans: (no idea, but could be 'not yet')

Nurse (who is also sporting the latest style in Covid-19 masks):
> *Eeenn oo thay ooenn oo thighnuth?*
> Trans: Didn't you say you went to Cyprus?

Me: *Ergh! Ooennin awthonah*
> Trans: Yes! You went in October

Patient: *Gggghhhnnnaaarrr*
> Trans: (no idea again)

Nurse: *Nahh munn thighnuth!*
> Trans: I love Cyprus!

And so on, and so on…

That final selling point on behalf of the rubber dam (stopping the patient speaking in anything vaguely resemblant of a known language) had a rather interesting side-effect.

Some husbands found it very useful, in that they didn't hear a word, not a single utterance, from their spouse for a good hour or so. I used to tell them I wouldn't charge for the treatment but they could pay me for the peace and quiet instead. You'd be surprised how many said okay.

Far more profitable.

***

Quite recently, I was treating the daughter of some very close friends of ours, a lovely girl who was known for being very talkative, when my mobile phone rang.

Normally, my phone is switched off during any treatment sessions, and tucked away in the pocket of my scrubs (because I have to keep counting my steps, don't I?), but this time it was sitting on the window sill by the open window (another Covid requirement — the open window, not the location of my mobile phone). As I wasn't actually 'in the mouth' at this precise moment, I sneaked a peek and saw the call was coming from my son.

Obviously, with any other patient in the chair, I would never have taken the call, but this young lady and this particular son practically grew up together because their mums spent a lot of time together, so I answered. Managing somehow to make my son understand what I was mumbling through my mask, I asked my patient if I could tell him she was with me, and once she had deciphered what I mumbled to her, she happily agreed,

I then switched the phone to loudspeaker and put it on the rubber dam, so the two of them could chat to each other.

To say the resulting scene was bizarre is a monumental understatement. As the nurse and I stood by and looked on, this pair managed to communicate — he on a mobile in London coming through my mobile on speaker and over the rubber dam, and she with her mouth clamped open with the rubber dam in situ.

I have to say, in over fifty years of dentistry, that was the first, and the only, such experience.

Ferrari Double Act

And now, to the matter of cars in the car park. I fully understand if you find this topic somewhat odd, given that you are reading a collection of dental-world memoirs, but I can confirm, without fear of contradiction, that both dentists and our patients do drive cars. And, very often, park them.

When I was working in our Quayside practice, at the point when I assumed my position to begin work on a patient, I had one window behind me and another to my side.

One day, as I was busy working on — and, we can only hope, concentrating on — a tooth, something caught my eye outside. At roughly the same nanosecond, something also caught my ear, and the two somethings belonged to the same object.

A gleaming, bright red Ferrari.

No normal human being could have missed either the visual spectacle, or the noise associated with it, as said Ferrari roared into and across our car park, followed by the screeching of brakes as it came to a very sudden halt about an inch from the fence. That's the fence forming a border around the car park, not some shady character in a gaberdine raincoat with the collar pulled up, wearing a trilby and dark glasses, nervously puffing on a Gauloise and glancing furtively in all directions.

Back to the Ferrari... the driver, a not-very-tall but immaculately dressed man, got out of the car, pushed the door shut (obviously, you don't need to slam the doors on a Ferrari), and then — forgive me if this seems even vaguely like stereotyping, and I assure you there is not a smattering of envy behind this comment — he assumed the posture that seems to be associated with drivers of the more glamorous and expensive motor cars. Throwing his head back as far as he could get it (but he still didn't look any taller), shoulders back and chest thrust out, he strutted — I can only describe his movement as strutting, because it wasn't a walk, a stroll or a meander — in the manner of someone who considers they are doing the world a huge favour simply by being in it, around the corner of the building (at this point I had to change windows to see him) and into our reception area.

I carried on working, hoping this had all transpired in a couple of seconds and that my patient hadn't witnessed any lapse of concentration on my part. Then, no word of a lie, not more than a few minutes later, the same thing happened again!

A second red Ferrari tore into the car park, screeched to a halt within an inch of the fence (that's still the boundary kind) right next to the first red Ferrari. Its driver got out — not a very tall chap but well dressed

— closed the door and assumed his stance. His head almost jolted back, his chest puffed out from the expensive suit, and he strutted round the building and, as I changed windows again, I saw him enter our reception area.

Now, the human brain does not like this kind of thing — you know, weird, almost unbelievable, and mine started searching for reason. Was there a Ferrari exhibition happening later on? Would there eventually be a whole long row of gleaming red Ferraris? Would they all screech to a halt scarily close to the fence (yes, still that fence)? Would they all have the strutting (possibly cloned) drivers?

Sometime later, (I'm not sure if I was still working on the same patient, or if I'd moved on to the next, but it's irrelevant) the driver of the first Ferrari strutted past my window (the one behind me, for your information), head high, shoulders back, chest puffed out, and rounded the corner (swift change of window), then he saw the two red Ferraris, side by side.

His Ferrari, and *someone else's Ferrari*.

If I'd hit him with a lump hammer, he couldn't have had such a sudden and extreme change of demeanour. His shoulders sagged forward, his head fell to his chest and he walked, ever so meekly, to his car, climbed in and drove, as quietly as a Ferrari can, out of the car park and out of sight.

Why? I hear you ask. Oh, the second red Ferrari, the one belonging to *someone else,* was a newer model.

No Hablo Español

A few years ago, pre-Brexit, when Britain was still part of the EU (in case things have changed even more by the time you read this, that's the European Union) and there was this thing called 'free movement of labour', which basically meant that anyone who was an EU citizen could work in any other EU country (provided, of course, that they could (a) find and (b) get a job — it wasn't a sort of freebie handout).

These rules and regulations always sound simple, and very rarely are.

I decided to instruct a local English-speaking Spanish lawyer (my Español was, and still is, next best thing to useless) to act on my behalf in registering as a dentist in Spain. The hoo-ha that ensued was staggering, and included having to send documents to the British Foreign and Commonwealth Office for them to stamp, but they didn't call it stamping a bit of paper — they called it Apostille. This is an official certificate issued by the government (in this case, Great Britain) to attach to the required documents in another country so that the other country will recognise the documents as valid without requiring any further proof. Simple?

The other aspect of processing an Apostille certificate (making it seem very special and important) is that the British Foreign and Commonwealth Office can charge eye-watering fees (per page, not per document). The signature of a local solicitor or notary (that's a posh solicitor) wasn't good enough for the Spanish. So much for being a member of the EU.

While this was going on, I looked for, and found, a nice little job — part-time and close to home (our home in Spain, not home in Manchester) with a local, but very Dutch, not British, dentist. Actually, there didn't seem to be very many Spanish dentists in this neck of the woods.

I would work with said Dutchman for a few days a year, whenever we were in the country, carrying out a specialist root canal service for him and for other local dentists, a few Spanish, some British and some of other origins. At the time, there were a lot of non-Spanish dentists working on the Costa del Sol, but I have no idea why. I can't think it was anything to do with the all-year-round sunshine.

Anyway, we agreed a start date, subject to my registration coming through. But this was Spain, and the dental authorities, just like everyone else in the country, had a very *mañana* attitude to — well, everything, really — and nothing happened quickly.

It took a whole year for them to decide I was a decent sort and someone they wouldn't object to plying his trade on Spanish soil. By this time, of course, someone else had been given the job — no doubt someone who had applied for registration at least a year before me.

Another suitable job was sourced and sorted, in a nice practice run by Nina, a young lady from the UK who specialised in crown and bridge work, so my endodontist skills fitted in well there and I started working for her. Unfortunately, (you knew something had to happen, didn't you?) her partner (as in, they were a couple, not a business partner or a dance partner or a bridge club partner), whose career was in the hospitality sector, had an offer he couldn't refuse to work in Dubai, and Nina decided to go and join him there. She couldn't sell the practice, so she closed it down. Once again, Yours Truly was out of work in Spain.

Not long after this disappointing, but still very hot and sunny phase, I decided I would register for work in Gibraltar.

This application went through smoothly and quickly (no *mañana*) and cost a mere £50 a year, whereas the Spanish registration cost somewhere between €500 and €600 *plus* the fee for professional indemnity, which, in the case of Gibraltar, came free, courtesy of my UK indemnity. Now that's more like a United Europe.

So, for a while, I worked in a practice situated above a restaurant (I choose my places of work very carefully) on Main Street.

While having lunch one day at said eatery, I started to feel rather unwell. I managed to climb the two flights of stairs back to the practice, only to be greeted by everyone telling me how really ill I looked. They rang for an ambulance. The advantage of being in such a small place is that emergency services tend to arrive most speedily, and equally speedily the ambulance personnel diagnosed a heart attack. Oh, heck. Still, I suppose, if you're looking for an upside it does prove that I have one (a heart, that is).

Since the building didn't have a lift installed, only a crotchety old out-of-service chair lift, and one of the paramedics was a rather slightly built young lady, they then rang for the fire brigade. As Gibraltar had managed to avoid going through a huge development programme in the few minutes since calling the ambulance, the fire engine arrived just as efficiently and I was soon being carried down the two flights of stairs (if I'd known, I could have just stayed on ground level) by two hulking great big firemen — I actually think one was a woman, but I was just glad of the lifting power — and taken to the main hospital.

At the time, Gibraltar had no cardiac surgery facilities, so I was carted off by ambulance to a private hospital in — yes, where else would it be? — Spain, and quite close to our apartment. I was told that, if this had befallen me before the border with Spain was re-opened, I would have had to be flown to the UK for treatment.

A little problem soon revealed itself... or let's call it a snag, or even a snag-ette (it was nothing huge). My hire car was parked in a hotel car park on the other side of the border, and Yours Truly, in normal fashion, had no idea what make, model, colour or anything else it was, and especially no clue as to the registration number. I couldn't even remember whereabouts in the car park I had left it.

The following day, we were supposed to be attending a family wedding on the coast (Spain, not Bournemouth), so my brother, his wife, and my mother were all there, which proved fortunate when my brother somehow managed to locate the hire car and fetch it — while I was in surgery, having four stents fitted in my recently rather poorly heart.

After surgery, which was kindly paid for by the Gibraltar government because I was working there (I suppose we should be thankful it wasn't Spain trying to navigate this logistical minefield, with more of their *mañana* attitude, or the hospital would still be waiting for their money), I had to be taken back to Gibraltar by ambulance so that the hospital where I'd been admitted could discharge me. My wife had to drive there, so I could then travel back with her to our apartment, which was still close to the hospital I'd just left. Oh, glory be! — the tangled web we weave...

My travel insurance meant I couldn't travel to the UK for the next ten days, so there we were, stuck in Spain with the never-ending sunshine (what a pain!)

and, even when I *was* allowed to go home (to Manchester, not to the Spanish apartment), instead of simply popping on an EasyJet flight that would take two hours and forty minutes to Manchester, oh, no, I had to fly BA to Gatwick, take a road journey to Heathrow, then fly BA to Manchester. Why spend less than three hours travelling after heart surgery, when you can cover the same distance in eight hours?

Oh, and I missed the wedding.

That Photo

You may remember a certain photo I mentioned, that was hanging in the waiting room of a dentist called David Blain (and he's still *not* the famous illusionist), and I bet you're absolutely desperate to find out if I ever did get a copy of it, or not. Talk about a cliff-hanger…

I told you I'd written to Ros, David's widow, and that she kindly replied, saying that, once she and their daughter, Susan, had everything sorted, she would get a copy to me.

Unfortunately, and very sadly, Susan died shortly afterwards, and I couldn't possibly bother Ros about something so — well, petty, really. Not long after Susan's untimely death, Ros passed away, too, and with her, my hopes of ever getting a copy of that dratted photo.

Some time went by, as it tends to do, and one day, while working in my surgery, I had a call from someone who turned out to be David's nephew, telling me he was joint executor, together with his brother, of the couple's estates. While sorting through some documents at the house, he had come across the letter I'd sent to Ros asking about the photo. He had tracked me down and asked if I'd like to go and collect the original framed picture. Would I? You bet I would!

As both nephews were from out of town and would only be around for a couple of days, I hastily shifted, moved and re-booked appointments, and generally transformed one very busy diary day into one very free and clear day, and dashed off to meet the two chaps at the house, full of renewed hope of finally getting my mitts on that coveted photo.

Alas, Fate was to disappoint me yet again. We hunted high and low, we searched every nook and cranny (whatever crannies are) and we turned the house upside down and inside out, but we came up with a big fat nothing.

Well, we did find *some* things, but none of them were even vaguely a group photo in a frame. One of the things we came across was a signed photo of one of dentistry's founding fathers, a chap by the name of G. V. Black. I did realise there was no way David and Ros could have met him, seeing as he had already been dead for many years by the time David went to Chicago… unless they met through some sort of spiritual medium, or maybe regressive hypnotism… but I digress.

This search was quite some task, because it appeared the Blains never threw anything away, and their time in Chicago was well documented by various items of memorabilia, such as travel tickets, timetables, and so on — and it appeared that Ros had her twenty-first birthday while they were in the States, a detail confirmed by the collection of congratulatory telegrams she had received (remember telegrams? Another one of those pre-internet technologies now regarded as almost Neolithic).

We have to bear in mind what a mammoth event their trip would have been — not like these days when you can just hop on a flight from Manchester and arrive in Chicago about five or six hours later.

They would have had to travel by road to Liverpool, board a passenger ship to cross the Atlantic to New York — a journey of some six or seven days — then catch a train to Chicago, taking another two or so days, making the total duration around ten days. And in present times, people moan like Billy-o (no idea where that comes from, but it's apt here) if they have to queue at the airport for a few hours! Oh, how times change. Or is it just humans?

During our MI6-type search for the elusive photo, we did unearth something very interesting.

Their house — the one we were taking apart — had been gifted to them by an uncle of David's who had made his fortune in the States (in oil, I believe) and who bought houses for all of his nieces and nephews in the UK. Where's an oil millionaire uncle when you need one? By the way, please keep that under your hat and never tell any of my nieces or nephews.

Anyway, what happened to the photo? I guess now it will probably never be found. However, in the spirit of my dear mother and her 'glass half full' attitude, I wonder if maybe Ros had taken it to a copying shop but just never had the chance to collect it before she died.

This next bit is what's known as a long shot. In fact, this one is a Long Shot, very long. If you, dear reader, own or work in a copying centre or instant print centre, and you have an uncollected photo dated around 1948, showing a load of newly graduated American dentists, would you kindly contact me at specialistendo@hotmail.com

I know it's a (really very) Long Shot, but if a miracle should happen, I will be eternally grateful, and happy to pay for the print as well. Thank you in advance.

Excuses — or are they *Reasons*?

Over the years, it has never ceased to amaze me (speaking as someone who is not easily amazed) how many weird and wonderful excuses (sorry — the patient is always right, so I should say *reasons*) people give for not showing up for their appointment.

I mean, rocket science it is not. You need dental treatment, an appointment is made, you turn up, the dentist does his thing and Hey, Presto! All is well in the world. Or at least, in your mouth (until next time you have dental problems, in which case we repeat the process — just in case you were in any doubt).

Let me entertain you with a selection from my vast collection of the reasons given for not turning up (the patients, that is — not me) ...

The surgery phone rang. *Ring-ring... ring-ring...* (It was the old days, when phones were real.)

On the line was a lady calling to say she would be late for her appointment. And the reason for her tardiness? Her helicopter hadn't turned up. *What?* Who goes to the dentist in a helicopter?

She explained — in great detail (a sure sign of feeling guilty) — that her husband, who was a builder (I'm guessing a very successful one) had chosen to live some fifty or sixty miles from Manchester, even though his business connections were all in the city.

His solution to this potential logistics minefield was to buy a helicopter. That, in turn, meant he had to own or rent a spacious piece of land suitable for the helicopter to land, take off and be kept when not in use — possibly an actual heli-pad. It also meant he had to employ someone who could actually fly the thing and, in this case, double up as his chauffeur of the more ordinary run-of-the-mill form of transport, his (no doubt very expensive and powerful) motor car. Or possibly even *cars*.

And so, the normal routine of this Mr Brickie-cum-Moneybags (no envy on my part, you understand — it's what I heard someone else call him) (honest) would be something along these lines...

The pilot (slash, chauffeur) would arrive at Mr B-M's home, fly him into Manchester to a (presumably) designated and (even more presumably) reserved parking area, where the helicopter would be left until its services were once more required.

Mr B-M and the chauffeur then take the car (with the chauffeur driving, because that's what a chauffeur does) to Mr B-M's office and off he would trot to do whatever it is a helicopter-owning, chauffeur-employing millionaire bricklayer does for the working day.

On this particular occasion, when Mrs B-M should have come for her appointment, the chauffeur was supposed to drive the car back to the helicopter, leave the car, fly the helicopter back to the B-M abode, collect Mrs B-M and fly her into Manchester back to the car, then drive her to — well, to us.

I fear all that dashing about, one minute up in the air, then down on the road, swopping in and out of two very different means of transport, and repeating the same journeys backwards and forwards in quick succession, picking people up and dropping them off, would make me quite dizzy. We can only hope, therefore, that someone who was legally licensed to be in control of a flying machine quite low over a city the size of Manchester did *not* suffer from such dizziness.

Anyway, it turned out that somewhere in among all of the flying, driving, parking, landing, taking off, to-ing and fro-ing, picking up and dropping off, something went badly wrong. I can't say I'm surprised. The end result of the wrong something was that Mrs B-M was going to be late. In fact, she might not make it to the surgery at all.

And all because a helicopter wasn't at her disposal (complete with the *not* dizzy chauffeur, I'm guessing) and clearly this woman knew nothing about a very commonly utilised service, widely available across the whole of the country, called taxis. I won't even mention public transport — let's face it, if your lifestyle resembles that of the B-Ms, you really are never ever, *ever* going to clamber aboard a number seventeen bus.

Not in a month of Sundays, as granny used to say.

***

Another patient — again, a lady — phoned one day to apologise for her impending non-attendance at the surgery, and her reason was that she couldn't get her car out through the property gates because there had been a power cut and the gates wouldn't open, not for love nor money.

Again, as with the aforementioned Mrs B-M, the thought of calling a cab didn't seem to enter her head — I mean, surely, she could have *walked* off the property via a manual side gate or some other means? And the cab would be waiting for her on the outside. Is it me?

And, just so I can use the word again, surely these gated communities, where the properties are expensive (putting it mildly) and each owner chips in for things like grounds maintenance (I mean, you'd have to keep those topiary peacocks properly trimmed, wouldn't you? — you don't want them looking like turkeys who've been for a night out on the tiles), security (and I don't mean the guy who works the door at the local lap dance club) and so on, *surely* they have someone like an estate manager who would be able to resolve undesirable situations such as power cuts — or he/she would be able to open the gates by switching them to manual operation…? Just a suggestion.

But, at the very least, why on earth didn't someone — *anyone* — ring the bloomin' power company?

***

And what about that time a lady (sorry, yes, another female) rang to tell us her husband had gone off with her keys when he left for work, and she was now locked in the house.

I suppose going off with the wife's keys is a lesser *faux pas* than going off with the au pair, but don't these people have spare keys?

It's a fact of life that we all lose keys. House keys, garage keys, car keys… and we all keep spares. It has to be one of the most basic aspects of common sense in everyday life.

I did start to wonder if he'd done it on purpose (you do read about these things, don't you?) but then my imagination ran riot and I turned this poor man, who was no doubt innocent and quite ordinary, into a powerful drugs baron… then he was an international arms dealer… so I had to stop myself and just accept that some people have no spare keys. And even less common sense.

***

In the late 1980s, the glittering world of dental surgeries adopted the practice of opening for business on at least one evening a week. This was an attempt to accommodate those patients who found it difficult, or even impossible, to attend during normal opening hours, to wit, mornings and afternoons.

Basically, we were trying to make it easier for our patients. With the benefit of hindsight, it appears that the more you try to help people, the more the people will extract the Michael. Which is pretty ironic, when all we were trying to do was extract their teeth.

Sadly, all we managed to achieve was the mass migration of some patients who, prior to this generosity on our part, would have had daytime appointments, who then made appointments for the evening session and, believe it or not, *still* didn't manage to turn up.

So, this incredibly innovative organisational scheme (well, we thought it was incredible and innovative) just turned into an anti-social weekly event for us, causing us to lose this portion of our social life. I mean, why would you want to be down the pub with your mates when you could be standing in your surgery gazing into someone's mouth?

Obviously, we couldn't fathom why any of our patients would possibly want to miss out on spending time with our fingers in their gobs, while they desperately attempted to respond to the obligatory questions we would roll out, such as *D'you have any holidays planned?* and *How's your boy doing at his new school?* We never asked anything vaguely interesting because, whatever the question, their answer would inevitably be *Argargarraragh*...

When we asked our receptionists about the peculiar phenomenon of the disappearing evening patients, we discovered that, in a lot of cases, the evening appointment had only been made earlier the same day, often in the afternoon. So, at some point during that small window of time, a mere speck in the cosmos, these people would completely forget the appointment they had only just made.

We never did discover the cause of this anomaly, but because science-fiction TV programmes and films were very popular at the time, we decided there must be a sort of fifth-dimensional wormhole in the fabric of local existence, and when our patients stood on a crack in the pavement, or walked under a ladder, they passed through the wormhole, causing any memory of dental appointments to be completely obliterated. Gone. Lost forever. Like some of our patients.

***

On the same subject, but with a variation on the theme, a number of patients (obviously quite a notable number, or I wouldn't have brought it up) would make an appointment and then just not turn up. No phone call, no apology, no excuse (sorry, I mean *reason*) — nothing. It was quite shocking. They remember they need the appointment, they remember how to operate their phone to call the surgery, they remember to ask for the appointment, then — total memory loss, apparently. They simply *forget* to turn up.

Come on, people. This is important. It's your health we are talking about, not to mention our income. It's not like forgetting to go shopping for new shoes, or forgetting to tell your next-door neighbour that your cat died last week.

Do you really want to ignore that bad tooth? It will only get worse, I promise you. And you'll have stinky breath. When you're in the pub with your pals and you lean forward to tell a rather rude joke, they'll all jolt backwards like they've been hit in the face with a plank of wood.

And you'll no longer be *Harry who's a great laugh* — no, you'll have morphed into *Watch out, here comes Harry Halitosis.* People will cross over the street to avoid having to talk to you, babies in prams will screw up their pink faces and scream loudly when you loom over them, and life will not be the same.

And, you'll have toothache. That endless, incessant pulsing pain inside your head that you can't ignore, that stops you getting to sleep or even relaxing. You can't eat or drink anything too hot, or too cold. No chilled lager after the footy for you, mate — no creamy latte at the office, no festive mulled wine… *and* you'll have to eat on one side of your mouth, but no matter how hard you try, sitting there with your head tilted at a stupid angle, one tiny bit of food will escape from the good side to the Bad Side and WHAM! Big pain.

And all because you 'forgot' your appointment.

***

During the '70s I worked in a dental practice where a very large proportion of our patients were immigrants and it soon became clear to me that different cultures dealt with making and keeping appointments in very different ways.

One typical example of this was when a patient had an appointment for Tuesday the seventh of the month but he didn't turn up. No phone call, just a no-show. Then, two weeks later, on the Tuesday, that patient would stroll into Reception, saying he had an appointment.

The receptionist would, obviously, check the appointments diary and discover that this patient's appointment was actually two weeks ago. When this was pointed out, his response was, *Oh, no, you said I must come here on Tuesday. Today it is Tuesday, so I am here.*

You can't argue with that kind of logic.

***

There was one really unusual situation that resulted in me not getting to see my patient, but, in this case, it wasn't the patient's fault.

My patient, a gentleman, was sitting in the waiting room and I was running to schedule, just finishing off with the patient before him. But when the nurse called this chap's name he seemed to have — well, disappeared. Not only did I not get to see him, I wasn't able to demonstrate to him my incredible skills.

We eventually discovered that this man heard his name being called so he stood up and the nurse beckoned him to follow her, leading him into the hygiene surgery, where he was asked to sit in the treatment chair. The next thing he knew, he was having his teeth cleaned and polished.

Presumably, he took it that this must be part of the process with a new patient, even though he'd been booked in with me for a consultation regarding his medico-legal case.

When the cleaning was completed, the chap left the premises without ever clapping eyes on me.

On investigation, we could see that his name was dangerously similar to the name of a chap who really *was* booked in for the hygiene session. Goodness knows where he'd got to. Because my patient had responded to hearing the name called, the nurse had no reason to doubt that she had the right person. And the patient, in his naïveté, had no reason to query what was going on.

It became evident on that day that you can run a dental practice on the basis of complete chaos and still manage to treat patients, even if the treatment isn't what they came in for.

***

Finally, something that has only happened to me (I can't speak for other dentists — I can only speak *to* them or *about* them) once in forty-nine years. A female patient, who really did *not* want to be in the dentist's chair under any circumstances, but who actually made it to the appointment, began talking before I managed to begin any work, and she carried on talking, asking me questions (but never waiting for me to answer) and relating various little stories about goodness-knows-what, and — I was totally shocked to realise this — she was still talking at the point where the session should have ended.

She had managed to use up the entire appointment without allowing me to even look in her mouth. Well, I couldn't possibly risk this kind of thing happening again, so I devised some rather clever techniques to use in the future, to avoid anyone else getting the better of me like that.

So, thank you, Jill (that's really her proper name) for teaching me such a valuable lesson.

***

After all these years in practice, suffering the infernal stream of late cancellations and no-shows, I think (and hope) I've actually found the perfect solution to this problem.

I've mentioned elsewhere my idea (okay, maybe not the most practical one I've had) of setting up a practice that makes appointments for patients, which are subsequently cancelled by said patients, and the patient receives a cancellation bill for a nominal amount, which he or she then pays.

Although brilliant, this plan did have the pitfall of some patients maybe not cancelling, and what then? So, I have now found a compromise somewhere between the two scenarios (because that's what *compromise* means): we charge a large — and, more importantly, a non-refundable — deposit, and this is a firm and unmovable arrangement (or is that just me?). No deposit, no appointment. And, just to tie it up in a neat bow, so to speak, we insist (oh, the power!) on at least twenty-four hours' notice of cancellation with a refund, or to make a new appointment.

And why not? It's quite common these days for a restaurant or hotel to take a deposit for a booking, so why shouldn't dentists? I bet you don't have a good answer — and, if by any chance you do, I don't want to hear it, thank you.

The great news (well, for me, it is) is that, since introducing this new (and pretty fabulous) scheme, how many no-shows or late cancellations do you think we've had? Go, on, have a guess... No? Okay, let me tell you — one. That's right, a single, solitary *numero uno.*

What's more, we never heard from that patient again — not even to ask for a refund!

And how many cancellations do you think we've had with a request for a refund? Guess, go on! No? Okay, you're pretty rubbish at this but I'll tell you anyway. It's another big fat *one*.

Problem solved. I have to say, I do ask myself — why didn't we do this sooner?

***

All of this thinking about patients *not* having treatment has led me to remember the father of a girlfriend I had way back in my younger days, a girl called Geraldine. Her dad was a local GP and he would often share with me his pearls of wisdom about the medical world, patients, and life in general. My favourite such gem was *Medicine would be a great profession if it wasn't for the patients.*

He was a very wise man.

A Very Taxing Time

This little snippet may be apocryphal, but as it's about a not-very-bright tax inspector, let's do it anyway.

A colleague of mine found himself hauled up in front of his tax inspector, to be grilled (they call it 'interviewed') about a certain aspect of his tax return. The inspector pointed out that HMRC hold on file details of average expenses relating to the operation of a dental practice, and said that his (the dentist's, not the inspector's) expenses were not within the accepted range of costs.

He (the inspector) did what all such officials do when they absolutely know they are right and you are absolutely wrong — he quoted from a document issued by one of the dental associations that listed all aspects of costs, from which he had concluded, most absolutely, that my colleague was doing something wrong. These people are like a dog with a bone (the officials, not the dentists).

However, my colleague took a deep breath, pulled his shoulders back and looked this chap square in the eye (not that anyone actually had square eyes), then explained, very calmly, that his figures *were* within the acceptable range of costs, and he suggested, most politely, that the inspector should take another look at the document — because he wasn't quoting from the correct section.

He (still my colleague, the dentist) went on to inform the (now seething) inspector that he (my colleague, not seething) was, in fact, the person responsible for compiling and producing said document on behalf of the dental association, and therefore he (my very calm colleague) should know better than — literally — anyone on the planet (or beyond).

I understand this grilling (sorry, interview) was brought to a very swift conclusion.

***

And on the same subject, here's another corker…

As most self-employed people will know (and if they don't, they'd better get ready, because it will happen), HMRC (Her Majesty's Revenue and Customs) — or, for our friends across the Pond, the IRS (Internal Revenue Services) — carry out random checks on the annual accounts submitted to them by businesses and self-employed people (those who pay taxes).

My turn to be selected for this special treatment came in 1985, when a letter arrived (sent either to myself or my accountant, I can't remember which, and in the Grand Scheme of this book, *ça ne fait rien*).

The letter, typed on headed paper proudly displaying the title *Inland Revenue,* the former name of this 'service', was informing us (both me and my accountant) that they would be carrying out an audit on my accounts. It included a phrase that has become quite famous (infamous) among the chosen masses — *we have reason to believe that you have not disclosed all relevant information.*

And there it began, what seemed an eternity of hell on earth in the form of having to deal with these people — people who, by definition, are undealable with. They don't listen, they don't understand, they don't discuss, they don't engage — in fact, they don't behave in any way like human beings...

I am now conjuring up a mental picture of a medieval factory, somewhere deep underground, dark and dank with the stench of brimstone and sweat, where enslaved demi-beings, their heavy chains clanging against the bare rock walls, clumsily construct little robots. Future tax inspectors.

Sorry... where was I? Oh, yes... there ensued a period of gross inconvenience and disruption to the business, lasting several months (the other thing these people don't do is *give up,* not ever).

It went like this: we would dig through our records and accounts until we eventually found something that could possibly be construed as an oversight or clerical error (name one business where this never happens — bet you can't) and we'd go back to the people from the Revenue with this tiny snippet, only to receive their robotic response every time, *We have reason to believe that you have not disclosed all relevant information.*

It was infuriating, to say the least. As I'm not known for saying the least when there is so much more that can be said, it was also annoying, frustrating, maddening, and probably many other adjectives with 'ing' at the end. *And,* it was really interfering with the running of the practice, not to mention interfering with my blood pressure. So, I won't.

Back and forth we went with this seemingly endless ping-pong game — we served with a little discrepancy from our records and they came back with their never-changing response, *We have reason to believe...* I'm not going to bother finishing that. It was a form of mental torture, like the ceaseless and monotonous dripping tap.

Every now and then, they would pose a proper question: one of these gems was, *We noticed that you spent a full week in America when the conference you were attending was only four days; was the rest of the week a holiday?*

As it happens, this was the conference in Phoenix, which you should have read about in amazing detail in *Beyond the Pond* (I've warned you before — there will be questions). The reason for the (ever so slightly) extended stay was that, in those days, the most economical travel tickets were available if you stayed for at least a week — stay less and you paid the forfeit. You'd think the taxman would appreciate such a sensible regard to business finances, wouldn't you? And you'd be wrong.

Eventually, after this tiresome game had dragged on for oh, so long, we had nothing left to offer them. Not even a miniscule potential query, absolutely zero. But still they came back with their dratted parrot-fashion *We have reason to ...* you know the rest. We requested to speak with the Tax Inspector, he who had sent these minions to disrupt the lives of hard-working folk, and our request was denied. We asked again. Again, refused.

At some point, my accountant managed to get hold of the actual Inspector, the one issuing the stuck-record *We have reason to...* Only on the phone, mind you, not in person — I wouldn't imagine this chap would ever put himself in such danger after driving people up the wall for months on end.

The accountant was met with an abject refusal to discuss the matter, but then, by some quirk of the universe, they discovered that they were both avid Manchester United fans, and that did it. Unflippin'-believable. The appointment was arranged for me to go to the Inspector's office in Manchester to discuss the issue (whatever the heck it was). After all we'd been put through — football resolved it. I believe this just served to strengthen my resolute stance over my Number One rule, SK *(Sport Kills)* — or, if it didn't, it should have.

During this ridiculous battle of wills, the Tax Inspector had requested (or was it *demanded*?) my appointment book, which, in those times was a ring binder with loose sheets of paper inserted, and appointments were written in pencil (because we very often had patients cancel and re-book, as I mention later elsewhere in this volume).

Anyway, there we were, in the meeting. I asked him to explain exactly what the problem was, because we simply couldn't find anything else to show him — because there really, honestly, seriously *wasn't anything*. He replied that the 'discrepancy' (his opinion) centred around a couple of days when I had not banked any cash. To explain, patients used to pay a contribution towards the cost of dental treatment, and this was normally cash. The implication here was, clearly, that I was not declaring this 'income' (still his opinion) for tax purposes, and that the 'money' (his unwavering opinion) had somehow found its way into my back pocket.

When I asked him precisely which days he was referring to, it turned out to be quite some time ago, and I *did* know why there was no cash banked for those two days. I was not the owner of the practice at the time, nor did I even work there! He had been looking at the appointment book dates relating to the previous owner.

Do you suppose, for one second, that I received an apology? Any offer of compensation for the months and months of disruption and time wasted? No. All I got was, *Thank you, Mr Cohen* (I wasn't 'Dr' yet, let alone Dr Dr), *I think that wraps it up. Good day.*

And I never heard from him again, ever.

All that, because he couldn't read the appointment book properly. It was some time after this, I was told that the Inspector who had the longest outstanding enquiry was made to sit with a toilet seat on their desk. In his case, a toilet seat was only just appropriate (my opinion, and I'm sticking to it).

Fanning the Flames

I'm not really sure how to put this without creating the wrong impression, but ever since I embarked upon my profession in dental practice, something seems to have repeatedly occurred in my life, a bit too often and a bit too close for comfort. That 'something' is fire.

Don't get me wrong — I'm no pyromaniac! I don't go around striking matches and dropping them into waste paper baskets, or casually lighting up a ciggie (not that I've ever smoked a single one — honest) while leaning against a petrol pump. I have no idea why fires have featured so much in my life as a dentist, but they have.

The most dreadful, frightening and devastating of these blazing episodes occurred in 2001, as you already know (it was the second of October, to be precise, as emblazoned in my memory), but more of this later. I'd better stick to telling these sizzling sagas in chronological order, otherwise you will be reading some twice while others could be lost forever.

First on this arsonous agenda (well, something or someone starts these fires — they don't just happen) took place when I was a brand-new dentist, with my first job in a proper practice that paid me the princely sum of

£60 a week. With all of this new wealth coming my way, I decided it was time I had a better car. I *deserved* a better car. I *must have* a better car, and it should be a new one. Not second-hand, not reconditioned, not even nearly new, but a shiny, no-previous-owners, this-year's-number-plated, no-mileage (well, apart from it being tested and delivered) *new motor car.*

This wasn't my first new car, technically speaking, but it was the first that was paid for by my new earnings, so it felt a lot more special. I really fancied the Ford Cortina GT (the Cortina was the forerunner of the Sierra, which in turn was the forerunner of the Mondeo — which is about to be discontinued). My wife, however, reminded me that, as a new father, perhaps a slightly less sporty version could be chosen. I just read that back and have to explain, it wasn't being a father that I had to be reminded of, honestly — I did remember being elevated to that status.

Having asked my dad about which dealerships to check out (and, equally, which to avoid, *know what I mean, mate?),* and, for once, actually listening to what he said, off I went to Nunn's Ford dealership in Salford, where, much to my joy and delight, I found a Ford Cortina — not the GT, just the standard model, but nonetheless *a new car!* And I bought it.

The dental practice where I was working was in a rather salubrious (not) suburb of North Manchester, called Harpurhey. To measure the level of salubriousness, this building was just around the corner from Bernard Manning's Embassy Club, so that should give you a feel for the type of neighbourhood of which I speak.

So, I would drive my lovely new silver-grey Cortina to work and park it in a side street a couple of minutes' walk from the practice. I say it was silver-grey but my memory of the colour may be a tad off, so please don't bother contacting me if you know differently. In the Grand Scheme, it's not that important.

One day, as I was working merrily away (or as merrily as things get in dentistry) on a patient, I overheard a conversation taking place in the reception area (being young and healthy, with extremely keen senses — not something I could manage today, believe me, with my hearing... or lack of).

Someone had rung the practice doorbell (sorry, that sounds like we had two doorbells, one to practice on and then, once you had become fully competent and mastered the skill of doorbell ringing, you could progress to the real doorbell — not true, of course) to enquire if anyone here owned a new Ford Cortina that was parked round the corner. With the mention of the word 'new', our receptionist, being one of the few individuals to whom I had not yet boasted about my *new* car, denied all knowledge and was about to send Someone away.

On hearing her words, I rushed from the surgery into Reception, shouting, *Yes! It's mine! I've got my Cortina parked there!*

I found myself staring into that high-eyebrowed, anxiety-ridden expression on the face of a total stranger (aka Someone) who responded with, *You'd better go and look, 'cos it's on fire!*

I raced round into the aforementioned side street, to find my brand-new gleaming dream machine (well, it was when I parked it) smouldering from under the bonnet.

One tow truck later, my poor car went back to Nunn's for repairs, having been told (me, not the car) the wiring loom was set too tight and the heat from the engine while driving had melted the rubber insulation, causing a short to the engine block. Yes, exactly what I'd thought.

***

A few years then passed by without further fire hazards, but then Fate intervened and the fires came thick and fast. And hot and smoky.

***

At the point when I was just setting out on my specialist career, a male colleague from London happened to be in the same situation, so we decided to take in as many endodontic conventions as we could, travelling together and sharing a room in whichever hotel was the venue for the event, thereby saving us both a bit of cash.

It was also good to have some company on these jaunts, especially someone I knew, and this chap was actually a schooldays best friend of my brother-in-law. Allow me to mention here that this arrangement was purely platonic, to make sure you are building the correct picture.

So, there we were, the two of us (platonically) in the city of Philadelphia, attending just such a convention.

Our hotel room was on either the fourteenth or the twenty-fourth floor. Purely for information, if you've never been in a particularly high building, it really makes no difference once you're up that high — it's all nose-bleed territory. So, there we were, on a level with clouds and low-flying aircraft, or that's how it seemed when you looked out of the window. And suddenly we were rudely awakened and being deafened by the ear-splitting sound of fire alarms bouncing off the walls.

Being so high up, we couldn't see what was happening outside, but in the reflection of the equally high-rise building opposite we could make out a lot of flashing blue lights, and the lights were attached to various emergency vehicles.

In an attempt to (1) not panic, (2) do the sensible thing, and (3) definitely not panic, we tried to call down to Reception on the hotel phone, but nobody answered. We tried again, and still there was no reply. This was a big hotel, with lots of guests and people to-ing and fro-ing, so surely there should be someone on duty at Reception? You'd think.

We opened our door and looked both ways along the corridor, left, then right, then left again, like a child was taught to do when crossing a road (and yes, that's the correct sequence — we were in the States). No one around, not a single person, and no sign or sound of anyone on our floor. Weird. We were told later that leaving our room was the worst thing we could have done if the emergency situation — the one about which we knew nothing — had still been ongoing.

Luckily for us, our increasing panic and the danger of breaking our rules (1) and (3) were abated when the alarms stopped, just as suddenly as they'd begun. As the building didn't seem to be collapsing under us, the flashing blue lights subsided and the vehicles they were attached to departed the scene in an orderly fashion, we decided to go back to bed — still separately and platonically, I might add.

We found out the next morning that, due to our jet lag, we had slept through the worst of the event, when the hotel had been completely evacuated. Completely, that is, apart from the two comatose Brits on the fourteenth (or twenty-fourth) floor. No one had thought to knock on any of the doors to check if any guests were still in their rooms. As we were both out for the count (separately and platonically), we wouldn't have known if they'd broken the door down and tipped us out of our beds.

And the cause of all this turmoil and trauma heaped on the two innocent British dentists newly landed on foreign soil? A tiny fire in the hotel kitchen, which was at least thirteen floors below us (and possibly twenty-three). This tardy information was small consolation for Yours Truly as I mentally re-ran the worst scenes from *Towering Inferno* and anticipated a heart attack.

No one was injured and the hotel was saved, which I was pleased to learn — once I'd calmed down.

***

As my expertise and experience in endodontics developed and expanded, the inevitable happened and I began to see my professional reputation spread into areas hitherto uninvaded by me.

A natural result of this new-found fame (not quite rock star status, but quite sufficient for a lowly dentist, thank you) was that I started to be asked to speak at many UK and overseas conventions and seminars.

In those dim, dark days of long ago, Powerpoint hadn't been invented, or thought of, and hadn't even existed as a glint in the eye of Bill Gates (in fact, Bill Gates probably wasn't even a glint in his father's eye at the time) and the then hi-tech method of giving a visual presentation to one's audience was via a Kodak Carousel projector. If, by chance, this arouses your interest, I am sure you can find one of these archaic machines in any reputable museum of technology.

Although the mighty Powerpoint refers to each digital image as a 'slide', in the Carousel era a slide was a small piece of photographic film contained in a frame made of cardboard or plastic, exposing within the frame the image area to be projected. Each slide was an individual and unique item (a bit like my good self, ha-ha!) and it was not normal practice to make any copies of these because that involved a rather lengthy and complicated procedure. Hence, these slides were valuable to us, and, more often than not, irreplaceable (again, like me).

One tiny example is the creation of a title slide with which to introduce the presentation. In the all-singing, all-dancing Powerpoint, you just type in the words and symbols you want, and *voila!* There you have it.

With the Carousel system, you had to construct the title, take a photographic image of that, have it developed and printed on to the slide film in a photography laboratory, then have the slide mounted in the frame. It's tiring, just explaining it.

All of the slides required for a presentation had to be loaded individually into what was called a magazine (please think *gun magazine*, and not your latest copy of *Men Only*), otherwise known as a carousel (you can tell that the art of product naming back then was a highly sophisticated and complex venture).

Each magazine held a maximum of eighty slides, and you had to remember to not only load them all in the sequence in which you wanted them to appear, but also upside down (the projector turned the image upside down, so to be correct on the screen they had to be mounted upside down in the magazine!). One slight distraction while doing this could mean having to remove every slide and re-load them all (often more than once). Depending on the presentation, some of us would use two projectors at the same time, running side by side, if, for example, you were showing 'before and after' images.

Anyway, there I was, giving this lecture in a London hotel, and I had two projectors running (that's two magazines with a total of one hundred and sixty slides, remember) when — RRRRRIIIINNNNNGGGGGG!!! (it's in capital letters to show it was very loud) — the awful sound of a fire alarm was attacking my ears, along with the ears of everyone in my formerly attentive audience.

Normally, in such cases, everyone just sits there, waiting to be told it's a false alarm, until somebody gets off their bum and goes to check.

Somebody did. It wasn't a false alarm — it was a real fire! We had to evacuate the building, right now, and leave *everything* behind. *NO!*

So, what did I do? I ran in the opposite direction to those people who *were* doing what they were told, as in evacuating the building, and I grabbed my two Carousels, desperate to carry them to safety without any of my priceless little slides falling out. I hugged them to my body like they were long-lost family, only less comfortable. These little things were my lifeline, the difference between me giving an interesting (I hoped) audio-visual presentation, and... well, just standing there, talking.

So, there we all stood, outside the hotel, and — of course — it was raining. And cold. Why is it *always* cold and wet when you have no choice but to go and stand outside — without your coat or umbrella? And there I stood, holding on to my Carousels for dear life, and trying to keep them dry — which, by the way, I wasn't able to keep myself.

Once we were all nice and wet, cold and fed up, the emergency was over and we were allowed back inside. The conference room hadn't been affected by the fire, so I was able to continue my lecture. Both Carousels and all slides safe and sound. And, unlike me, quite dry.

***

A lot of people actually think about what they would do if their house, or their business, was suddenly engulfed in fire. And the big question is, given that you'd have no time at all to spare, what would you grab as you ran screaming from the building?

There are the obvious answers, of course. The kids (I hope this would be top of your list), the dog (or cat or canary or — if you are inclined towards the more exotic — your pet alligator), your wallet, bag, mobile phone, laptop or briefcase — or all five of these if you're a twenty-first-century Super-Mum who (while looking like a world-class model fresh from the beauty salon) juggles children, the home, business, the gym, charity work, fundraising coffee mornings and wine with the girls.

The truth is, when you're facing potentially roaring flames that will soon be licking at your flesh, you don't think sensibly. Not anywhere close to sensibly. You can't even see 'sensibly' in the rear-view mirror...

When our youngest son was around four or five years old, the three of us took a little break and stayed at a rather nice hotel in Newcastle — that's the upon-Tyne version, not the under-Lyme one (please note, I'm not suggesting for one nano-second that Newcastle-under-Lyme doesn't have a very good hotel, or probably several... please don't send me letters or emails).

So, we were having our little family break (it was a little break and we were a little family in case you are wondering which word the adjective applied to); I believe this would now be referred to as a *staycation,* and I cannot be held responsible for other people messing with our language, so please don't contact me about that, either.

At the time, I was on a diet, one of many fads I kept trying in my attempts to lose weight and get fit. This one was the Cambridge Diet, which consisted of some awful powder mix that was supposed to replace a proper breakfast (the very sight of the stuff made you yearn for fluffy scrambled eggs and grilled tomatoes on golden toast...) plus a diet bar that looked a bit like a Mars Bar, for lunch. Believe me, looking like a Mars Bar does *not* make these things taste like one.

My son and I were sitting at the bar (I promise I was *not* feeding him any alcohol, honestly). He was waiting eagerly for his toasted cheese sandwich, and I was, definitely not eagerly, dreading having to consume yet another of my diet bars, when — shock, horror! The fire alarm went off.

As mentioned previously, everyone just stayed where they were, assuming this was a false alarm. But then someone from the hotel management rushed in and ordered us all to evacuate the building — without stopping to take anything with us.

What did I grab? I can hear you saying it. You're thinking I must have scooped up my little boy, and yes, I did. But only after I'd grabbed my diet bar. Then I ran, as if the devil were after me. Something I could do back then. Not because of the faddy diets, just because in those 'back then' times, I was younger.

***

Early last year, I was staying in a hotel in Nottingham and, just as I was getting ready for bed, the fire alarm shattered the silence. Unfortunately for me, I had taken to sleeping *au naturel* (something I eventually stopped doing when my youngest grandson found out and said, *Ugh! That's gross, Grandpa!*)

As I said, the alarm sounded and it was time to grab something before scurrying out of the building with all the other guests. So, what did I go for? A dressing-gown? There wasn't one. A coat? Didn't think of that. Big mistake. My phone? Of course. And a towel.

This towel was, in the opinion of the hotel marketing people, a bath towel. In my opinion, humble or otherwise, it was a large hand towel. I wrapped it around me and headed downstairs, to be met by a most amused assortment of guests and staff. Worse, because I was a regular at this particular establishment, the staff never let me forget the incident. Not ever.

***

Before Covid-19 existed in our lives, the British Endodontic Society, of which I am a long-standing member, would hold its autumn meeting at a venue chosen by the incumbent President. As I was bestowed with the honour of holding that lofty position one year, I plumped for a spa hotel in the Midlands.

It was regular practice for spouses (or now you'd say 'partners', or — better still — 'life partners') to accompany the members, and they would 'do their own thing' while the formal business was being conducted, but on one evening we would all get together for a splendid dinner with an invited after-dinner speaker. This person would normally be non-dental and, hopefully, entertaining.

My wife and youngest son (by now a teenager, and nobody ever sees that coming) were with me and, as we expected, our boy had no interest whatsoever in the dinner, so off he went to do — well, whatever.

The dinner was going well and was about halfway through when — yes, you guessed it — the fire alarm went off. Oh, what joy! And all that good food still to be eaten. Once again, we all just stayed where we were, assuming it wasn't for real, and waiting for a person of the management variety to advise us one way or the other. That didn't take long, and one such bod appeared, somewhat hurriedly, and told us we must evacuate the building. Now. And, of course, we must not stop to gather any of our belongings.

I know I don't need to say this, but when we got outside, we found it was very cold — and, of course, raining. Well, it was autumn, I suppose. My wife, having gone to some lengths to glam up for the dinner, was concerned about her hair — more so, in fact, than any concern for the building being burned to the ground.

Suddenly, it hit us both — where was our son? He wasn't here, outside with everyone else, and we definitely couldn't go back inside to search for him. Hair worries were thrown to the winds (my wife's, not mine), we searched around frantically for the missing teenage offspring, hearts in mouths, until we found him with one of my colleagues, a lady who told us she had found him outside his room in the corridor, wondering what he should do when the alarm sounded. Relief!

Panic over, pile of ashes averted, we all went back to carry on with dinner.

We never did find out why that female colleague was in the hotel corridor, when she was supposed to be at dinner with the rest of us, but the main thing was that everyone was safe and well in the end, so we let that go. (Still, it was a bit odd.)

Something just struck me, due to sitting here, writing about all of the various fire episodes in my life — on two of these occasions, our youngest son was present. I wonder, could there be a connection…?

***

A few weeks before writing this, I was working in a dental practice in Nottingham when — seriously, do I need to say it? — the fire alarm went off. The same question enters my head every time (and I'm pretty sure it's the same for others): is this real, or is it just a false alarm?

Fortunately, I had just finished working on a patient when we were told it was a *real* alarm, that there was a *real* fire, and that we *really, really* had to evacuate. Grabbing my phone, I went straight outside, joining the others to stand in the cold and the rain. And wearing only clinical scrubs.

By the way, in my opinion, for what it's worth, there are only three things that are important enough to justify being grabbed in such dire circumstances, and they are: passport, wallet, mobile phone. Anything else is replaceable, and certainly not worth risking life and limb for.

***

Of all my tales of fires, I am about to tell you of the worst scenario I experienced. This is The Biggie.

October the second, 2001. Having arrived home late that day, I was sitting, eating my dinner and reading the newspaper. My wife was watching TV in another room, and our younger son was upstairs in his bedroom. I would point out that he was *back* living with us, and not *still* living with us.

Suddenly, he was tearing down the stairs, shouting (a bit disappointing, considering we taught him not to run on the stairs, and not to shout in the house). Parenting is not an easy hobby.

Dad! he yelled, *somebody just phoned to say your practice is on fire!*

Oh, don't be silly, I replied, ever so calmly, *I would have heard from Phil if that was true.* Phil was my business partner and his name was first on the list of emergency contacts for our practice.

No, Dad! Really! It was somebody who knows one of the fire assessors and he says it's definitely your place!

I admit I was now (a) confused and (b) a bit worried. Why hadn't I been contacted if this were true?

Okay, I'll call Phil and see if he knows anything.

Phil didn't. That made two of us. He agreed that it was strange neither of us had been called, and now there were two of us worrying. We agreed that the best thing to do was call the security chap in the car showroom opposite the practice, as they had twenty-four-seven security on their premises. No luck getting through to him, so we moved on to Plan B, to call the bar next door to our place. The owners knew us — not because we were rowdy, heavy-drinking revellers, but because we regularly held our practice meetings there (with non-alcoholic drinks, of course).

I managed to reach one of the bar staff and asked her if she knew what was happening.

No, sorry, I don't know anything about it, but it does look like there's a lot of fire engines outside with their lights flashing.

No comment.

I rang Phil, quickly updated him and we agreed to meet at the practice. I told my son what was happening, gathered up my keys and coat, and popped my head round the door to tell my wife. *I'm just off to the practice — it's on fire — speak to you later,* and I dashed for the front door.

Okay, see you later, she said casually, then, after a silence of a split second, she shrieked, *WHAAAAAT? What did you say?*

Almost through the front door, I called back to her, *Practice on fire — got to go!*

I'm coming with you!

The pair of us jumped into the car and I drove the four or five-mile journey, only to find the road blocked by police and fire vehicles and personnel, like a scene from one of those intense TV crime dramas that get you really on edge, then, half an hour later, everything is fine again. A quick explanation of who we were, and they let us through, to be met by a very upsetting scene of flames leaping all over the place from our beautiful two-storey Georgian/Victorian/Edwardian (never did find out which) building, and a lot of firemen rushing around.

The firemen were concerned that someone could have been inside the building, even though it was now nine in the evening. We told them we didn't know when the cleaners came in, so it was actually possible that one of them could have been in there. So, we rang the security alarm company, who told us the alarm was showing 'open', which would mean the alarm hadn't been set, and that meant there was a strong possibility that someone was inside. I felt sick.

For some reason that escaped me then, and still does, once the fire was dealt with (as in, it was out) the fire crew persuaded us to go into the building — yes! that's what I said, *they* persuaded *us* — to see if we could find any sign of the cleaner.

WHAT? I still, to this day, have no idea, not a smidgen of an idea, not even an idea of an idea, why the firemen didn't go in. They had all the gear, the helmets, gloves, boots, breathing apparatus (as you'd expect, because they were firemen) ... we had our coats over normal clothes and didn't look anything like firemen.

I reckon it was because we were in shock, but we just did it. We went in to a building that had just been gutted by fire, and we looked for a cleaner. You couldn't make it up. Happily, there was not the slightest trace of a cleaner anywhere.

There was no trace of several other things — like the staircase, the soft furnishings and most of the interior. We found out the next morning that the alarm system showing as 'open' actually meant the alarm had been set, therefore nobody was going to be in the building. Pity nobody thought to explain that before we walked into the charred remains of our workplace.

Phil and I both had one major thought rattling around in our heads. The records of all our patients, records kept in the building. Remember, this was way before the Cloud and all that tecky stuff. The files were stored on the server, which was located in the exact opposite corner of the building to where the fire had raged. Taking our turn at the persuasion game, we got one of the firemen to go in, find the server, unplug it and bring it to us. I swear, I never saw anyone move quite so quickly (and unwillingly) as that chap did, but he delivered the server to us so we were happy about that.

Phil spoke to the computer supplies people and they came along the next day, and they fortunately managed to retrieve all of our data from the rather toasted server. Oddly, the second all of the data was transferred safely, the hard drive seized completely, never to function again.

Realising we needed to get a base camp set up quickly from where our two receptionists could operate, we agreed that my study at home would be the best option until things could be sorted on a longer-term basis.

Phil called all the staff to let them know what had happened and that they should wait for a call from us when we could tell them more. Of course, all patients had to be contacted, lists had to be compiled of all items destroyed for the insurers, and a thousand other things that go with such a disaster.

Phil and I went back to the old building the next day, after we both suffered a rather sleepless night, and we found that a structural engineer had declared the building unsafe. Bulldozers arrived and reduced our once glorious practice to rubble and dust.

It was lucky that we had no appointments booked for the next day (it was a Jewish holiday), and the only thing in the diary was an interview with a dental nurse. She didn't turn up and we never heard from her again. Maybe she'd heard about me and fires.

By the way, I have just driven past the old site and the landlord has erected a *huge*, and I mean *MONSTROUS*, development of apartments on the site, together with the site next door, which back then was the afore-mentioned bar.

A Word About Nurses

I know I've touched on the subject of nurses previously in this volume (I said the *subject,* I've touched on *the subject* of nurses, not the nurses — what are you people like?) and you know that, since I've been in practice, I've never worked without the aid of at least one dental nurse because their assistance in the surgery is invaluable.

In the States, these people who assist dentists are known as... erm... well, they are known as dental assistants, which to me seems a much better title for them, because they *assist* in the world of the *dentist.* But what do I know? (Don't answer that, please.)

My wife always says that, whenever I'm doing any jobs at home (I admit that's not very often, but obviously it's often enough for her to comment), I insist on having an assistant (not a dental one, that would be a waste of their special skills) and she puts this down to the fact that I always have someone assisting me at work — my right-hand man, as it were.

To be absolutely accurate (you should know me well enough by now, if you've been paying attention), being right-handed myself, the assistant is actually my left-hand man, even though all the nurses I've worked with have been female so it should be my left-hand woman (I'm never sure where the line is between being accurate and being pedantic). In aviation parlance (as you know, I'm bilingual), the nurse would be the dentist's 'wingman'.

For the sake of clarity, I will refer to my assistants as *nurses* in this chapter and beyond, but if you are reading this in any country other than the UK, then you may translate that to suit (I'm definitely not shutting the door to any global sales).

It has been calculated (properly, with maths and everything) that dentists spend more waking time with their nurses than they do with their wives, and it has to be said (although definitely not in my case, please note) that some dentists take this a little bit too much to heart, or whatever part of the anatomy comes to mind. Better stop there, I reckon.

One of my nurses in the '80s (that's the 1980s, not that she was in *her* eighties) and her husband were friends with my wife and myself. She used to say that I worked for her, and I have to say there may be more than a grain of truth in that statement, even if it was meant as a joke.

Because of the close relationships with nurses, there would inevitably be a history of associated anecdotes. Digging into my own chronicles of dental history, over the past forty-nine years I've worked with literally dozens of nurses, and I am sincerely grateful to them all for their hard work, commitment and —

perhaps more importantly — for putting up with me. I can't pay homage to all of them here, but there are four who I would like to mention, as they were instrumental, albeit not exclusively, in my development as a dentist.

By 1978, after two years of learning better root treatment techniques, practising on my own patients (as opposed to pinching them from other dentists), and taking a few referrals from fellow dentists through our local Jewish Dental Society (they knew about my enlightenment, my Eureka! moment, at their meeting in October 1976), I had the confidence to move on to a bigger city centre practice, as in a bigger practice, not a bigger city.

Discreet enquiries were made, because that's how we did it in those days — no shouting from the rooftops, telling every Tom, Dick and Harry your business — and I moved to a most reputable six-surgery practice (quite a sizeable place back then) and this was my introduction to private dentistry. Although I didn't realise it at the time, it was also to be a lesson in *real dentistry*, not that I had been faking prior to this.

After being there for a while, in a part-time capacity because I still had my own practice in the suburbs, I started working with an amazing nurse who we called Big Jan. We had another Jan at the practice, and she was known as — wait for it — Little Jan. Please don't think these two ladies found the nicknames inappropriate, as I can assure you, they were both happy with their soubriquet and it was simply that one of them was tall and the other was — well, not tall.

Big Jan had worked for one of the senior partners for a number of years and had picked up a great deal of dental knowledge from this chap. He and his brother, also a senior partner, became great mentors to me when I later undertook my research degrees. Both were extremely talented dentists, and had an invention under their belt (not literally, as it was to do with dental work) — a novel method of restoring teeth that had broken down quite badly. Yet another invention appearing in my immediate circle. Spooky.

Working with Jan was very instructive, as she was more than happy to pass on her knowledge gleaned from working with other dentists. With some people, trying to get them to impart any useful information is like pulling teeth — in my case, literally. To this day, I still say I learned more dentistry from Big Jan than I had gathered from my five years in dental school.

Little Jan was younger and less experienced than her namesake, but just as intelligent, and keen to learn and assist. At the time, Phil and I used to run post-graduate courses in various hotels around the country, and on those courses was a section in which I wanted to teach the procedure of using the rubber dam. You have read a little about this earlier, but here's more.

Although it may sound like something a family of rubber beavers might build, it's actually a sheet of rubber used to isolate a tooth during treatment. In those days, it wasn't widely used (well, no wider than a patient's mouth) but today it would be seen as neglect if we didn't use it — in case anyone from the higher authorities should be reading this, I am definitely not negligent.

I asked Little Jan if she would come with us on the courses to teach the application of the rubber dam to dentists — I knew she could do it because she'd seen it done so many times and clearly understood the whole process.

Straight away, she agreed and seemed keen, even if only to do some extra paid work outside of the surgery, but when it came to the first evening of the course, she suddenly had a wobble (not a comment on her physique, I promise) when she realised what she had let herself in for. I tried to reassure her, and told her she certainly knew more about the rubber dam than any of the dentists on the course. Even though she didn't believe me, she agreed (phew!) to give it her best shot. About five minutes in, she sidled up to me and whispered, *You're right — they don't know anything!*

After that, for the rest of the courses it was downhill all the way. Well done, Little Jan.

Not long after my time with the Jans, I began working with (for) Claire. By this time, I was only working in one practice and was only doing root canals all day, so Claire soon picked up on what endodontics was all about. One day, she asked me, *Dr Cohen,* (it was all very formal in those times when addressing anyone with a doctorate or whatever) *why is it that sometimes it takes you four minutes to find a root canal and forty minutes to clean it, whereas other times it takes forty minutes to find one and only four minutes to clean it?*

I was stumped, and that's an understatement. I had no idea how to answer. So, in true PhD graduate style, I referred to the literature... nothing. In fact, less than nothing.

Because of this question, I think I eventually rationalised it by redefining the way root canals react to inflammation... I could carry on explaining, but (a) it's not entertaining if you are not in the world of dentistry and therefore (b) you'd be bored. Bored is something I definitely don't want you, dear reader, to be, so I'll move on.

In brief, it led me to understand something that I had formerly not realised, which in turn helped me in my work. And it was all down to Claire, my nurse.

I must also tell you about Danielle. As far as I remember, Danielle came to us straight from school, a bright girl and very socially aware. One thing I learned as a dentist is that I can spot a potentially good nurse early on (and probably at fifty paces) and in her case, I saw that she would be capable of working with/for me, so when my then current nurse left, I offered Danielle the post. She accepted.

Apart from being a good endodontic nurse, Danielle possesses one characteristic that I had rarely seen in a nurse — her innate ability to predict what I was going to do next. And, strangely, often before I'd thought about it.

I well remember one occasion when I was working on a particularly difficult tooth (there weren't any *not* difficult teeth, they were all just different degrees of difficult — very, terribly, incredibly... and that's why we charged so much) and I couldn't decide what to do next.

Various scenarios ran through my head until I decided to try an instrument that we hardly used, and I was just about to ask Danielle to get it for me when I looked up from my microscope to find her hand proffering the very thing. A rare talent, indeed.

Or maybe Danielle really was psychic...

High Tea (or Lunch... or maybe Dinner)

Have I mentioned before that I have a bit of an issue with heights? I'm not sure if I told you or not. I'm not sure about a few things these days, truth be told.

I don't mind being up high in a building, as long as I'm not near the outer walls where there's a window and you can see straight down, as in absolutely vertical. I can look out, standing back a little way from the window, into the distance (the further, the better), which means I'm perfectly okay to fly my plane — I know people find this odd, but it does work.

What I *can't* do is look straight down from a height, and any attempt to do this brings on a very sudden, and very strange, sensation: my legs go weak, my knees wobble (not literally, but that's how it seems) and I feel really weird — it's one of those experiences you can't find a proper description for. And, as soon as this whatever-it-is overwhelms me, my mind starts to conjure up all manner of negative images and scenarios — I'm falling over but without landing, just continuous falling, down, down, all the way down... or the building I'm in starts toppling and collapsing... Not good.

Not minding actually *being* up high (without looking at the sheer drop, thank you very much) involves *getting* up high in the first place (obviously) and this in itself can be a problem. I can use a lift (or, if I'm in the States, I can use an elevator), as long as the lift is on the *inside* of the building. The very sight of those external all-glass goldfish bowls skimming up and down the outside of incredibly tall buildings gives me the heebie-jeebies.

I have a question.

Why is it that some of the best restaurants are always situated up in the clouds on the very top floor of the building? Why not the basement? I suppose the view from the basement isn't quite as breath-taking as from God's corridor; actually, in a basement there wouldn't be a view of any description... maybe, if there was a window at the very top of the wall, you'd see people's ankles and shoes as they walked past. Not quite the glorious cityscape you'd expected.

I guess I just answered my own question, in which case at least I know I have an intelligent response (joking). So, that explains the high-altitude location of the posh eateries where you are given an oxygen mask on arrival. It's the stunning view — and I bet they consider that when they come up with the prices for the miniscule-portioned menu.

When I'm in an area I've never previously graced with my presence, I do choose such a place to eat, the restaurant where I can enjoy the most panoramic expanse of cityscape — but I won't have a window table. I'll enjoy my view from further inside, if you don't mind, so I can gaze into the nether yonder of buildings, parks, roads, rivers and whatever else is on offer, and not have to scare myself silly with the sheer-drop aspect.

During all of those USA trips I made to attend various conferences (or conventions, as my American hosts would call them — just in case this volume goes international), it was the done thing for all the Brits to stick together, especially when eating in the evenings. Remember, they have dinner when we are having our afternoon tea.

Anyone who has visited Seattle will be familiar with the Space Needle, where the restaurant is located some five hundred and eighteen feet up from ground level. In Toronto (yes, I know that's Canada — don't be so pedantic), the CN Tower stands (goodness knows how) one thousand, eight hundred and fifteen feet high. A vertigo sufferer's nightmare.

When I got together with my fellow British colleagues in both of these places, where do you suppose they had decided we would eat? Yep. Got it in one. Or should that be two? Then, to make this an even more joyous occasion for Yours Truly, when we arrived at each of the sky-scraping structures, there, in front of us, in all its high-tech-design glory, was an external glass lift.

I had no way out (and no other way in). I think I managed to hide my terror as I entered the goldfish bowl, thankful for being in a group and constantly shuffling to keep myself in the centre of said group. I stood with my back to the outside world, as it whizzed past in a downward blur, and avoided moving my head so that I was looking at the building for the whole vertical journey. Once in the restaurant, I made sure I sat facing *into* the room.

When I worked in Singapore, tall buildings were all around, and impossible to avoid. Fortunately, most of them had internal lifts. Phew!

Along with two colleagues (actual real Professors) I'd been invited by the Singapore government's Ministry of Health to give two weeks of presentations to an eager group (one can live in hope) of qualified dentists of varying levels, up to and including the dizzy height of consultant. This could be a tricky audience.

Our chief host, and the organiser, was a consultant orthodontist at the main government hospital. On the first day, after introducing each of us to the 'students', he added that, as we would be working hard from early morning, our hosts would take us out for a late lunch, and a rota would be arranged with choices of restaurant. It came as a relief to Yours Truly that they had taken on board my requirement for a vegetarian diet, so all eateries on the rota had to cater accordingly.

I have to say we were taken to the most amazing places and we ate really well. After being fed and watered in style, we were then free for the afternoon and evening. I use the word 'free' loosely. We still had to get together with my boss to plan the lecture schedule for the following day (if this was a panto, you'd boo now); then, having sorted that, we three had to go back to our own rooms (not the 'boss' cos he organised the 'get-together' in his room — of course) to plan the details of our actual individual lectures (more booing, please).

I think (but don't hold me to it, as I've slightly lost track of what I've written now) I've told you about the old Carousel projector and image slides being the forerunner of today's PowerPoint and flash drives. Lugging a projector and a collection of slides around was a pretty Herculean task, compared to carrying a tiny memory stick in your breast pocket, the size of a small tie clip. The sad thing is that the stick can hold more information. That's called progress.

For this particular trip, I had taken over a thousand slides (yes, that many) and, in a vain attempt to make carrying and setting up somewhat easier, I had a special briefcase for the slides and this item went everywhere I went, except the loo, of course. On this occasion, I carted it around for four weeks; I didn't even check it in as luggage, I just kept it with me. I'm sure, looking back, that I started to develop real pecs...

Anyway, back to the story. Our hosts decided to hold a formal dinner (formal, as in I had to find a shop where I could buy a long-sleeved white shirt because the summer wear I had packed just would not do) in a private dining room in a restaurant at the top of one of the tallest hotels. Thirty-eight floors up. I can feel the blood draining from my face as I write.

The host of this particular event was Singapore's Permanent Secretary for Health, who happened to be the brother-in-law of the Prime Minister (theirs, not ours), so the invitation could *not* be refused. In accordance with my heights problem, I trotted off to carry out a pre-dinner recce to check out the lift situation. Thank heaven (the exact location of the restaurant), the lift was happily inside the building. I mean I was happy, not the lift.

When we gathered in the cloud-level venue, it turned out that I was the one and only veggie, and the host had arranged a special menu for me — and it was printed on a proper menu card. Just for me. I started to suspect that this chap must have me confused with someone incredibly important, but the special menu was helpful for me to understand what I was eating — when you are veggie, people often go overboard with the complexity of dishes to impress you and you end up gazing at a bowl of something you can't identify. It's quite worrying.

Worry averted, and for that I thank the people of Singapore for their courtesy, hospitality and consideration.

We sat at an enormous circular table, with a matching Lazy Susan (you know you're somewhere posh when the spinning bit matches the standing-still bit), and our host (the Very Important Person) insisted on sitting next to me so he could serve me my food from the rotating display of edible delights. We got chatting and I found out he was a retired senior consultant haematologist (that's the blood area of medicine); he was father of the consultant orthodontist (our organiser) as well as brother-in-law to the Prime Minister at the time, Lee Kuan Yew, the founder of modern Singapore, the man who achieved the country's transition from third world to first world.

Just to prove that I am perfectly at home when in the presence of such noble dignitaries, when he had done a great job of serving my food, I told him if he ever gave up his day job, he could be a waiter. My colleagues overheard me. They were, to put it mildly, horrified.

Technology, not Toothbrushes

For some years now, I've been volunteering in my professional capacity in a clinic for deprived children — in Israel. Jerusalem, to be precise. Well, if you're going to help out, why not do it where you're needed the most? And Israel's nice this time of year.

This clinic accepts children for dental treatment who are referred from a variety of agencies, and it doesn't matter what religion each child or their family follow. They also make sure that any dental work beyond general treatment is carried out by a relevant specialist. You can see why I admire and support this place. So, most of the treatment is carried out by general dental practitioners — these people come from all around the world to help out — and root canal treatment is carried out by an endodontist, in this case being Yours Truly.

When my wife and I first took the trip to Jerusalem so I could work there, we found a decent hotel nearby where she felt comfortable, content to enjoy the day on her own while I was at the clinic. After all, happy wife, happy me. We had hired a car at the airport, and I used it to get to and from the clinic each day — even more reason to make sure Mrs C was content in her surroundings, as she couldn't really go anywhere.

This hotel had an underground car park but when I studied the tariff, the charges seemed a bit pricey (does that make me come across as a bit mean? I'm not, honestly) and anyway, I'd seen some parking bays outside the hotel with pay-as-you-go meters. The meters appeared to be of the not-currently-working type (again, this is *not* me being stingy, I promise), so — I know this is not going to help my case — I left the hire car overnight in one of these bays.

Nothing happened as a result of this rather questionable parking (as in, I wasn't arrested), so I carried on using the bays every time we stayed at this hotel, and I never needed to pay for parking (oh, flip! There I go again — seriously, this is not me being miserly).

One morning, arriving at the car in its regular space, I found — shock, horror! — there, on the windscreen, a parking ticket! I had no idea what I was supposed to do with this, but I did fathom how much the fine was that I now needed to pay.

The next day, I tried to use the parking meter and — surprise, surprise — the instructions for using it were all in a foreign language (I realise this is a stupid comment, seeing as we were in a foreign country). It wasn't just the actual language, but the alphabet making up that language was a very far cry from the A to Z of home soil. If you looked at these symbols and screwed your eyes up a bit, they were like musical notes written with a thick black felt-tip pen.

You'd think I should have seen this coming, but I have a sneaking suspicion that we Brits expect that every country in the world (and probably beyond) will cater to our every need, and have any information they wish to bring to our attention written in good old English. Well, it ain't so.

Anyway, completely overpowered by language, alphabet, parking meter and instructions, I decided to put the car in the underground car park overnight, even though it was going to cost a bit.

In the morning, I asked at Reception how I could pay for the parking before I drove the car out (thereby avoiding the possibility of making it seem that I was doing a runner) and I was informed, very politely, that parking was, in fact, free to all hotel guests.

So, for several years, I'd been risking being given multiple parking fines, when all I had to do was read the hotel's parking instructions properly to realise that I could enjoy free parking. I don't think I've ever before or since made something so simple so bloomin' complicated.

There's something I was really shocked to discover whenever I visited this clinic, relating to the children themselves. Bearing in mind that each and every one of these youngsters is suffering deprivation in some form, and they are referred to the clinic by any of the official agencies working with children in need, such as social services, children's homes and so on, some of them have *never* owned a toothbrush. Those who may actually have one could be sharing it with an entire family, or the brush could be years old and useless.

But, to this day, I have never seen a child there who didn't have a mobile phone with them. What a sign of the times, when a mobile phone is more important than looking after your teeth.

What's more, they all want to use their phones for social media — even when I'm actually treating them! Many's the time I've had to ask them to put the phone down so I could get into their mouths — sometimes when I'm drilling!

The Slippery Slopes

Regrets… I've had a few… but honestly, *very* few.

One, however, is that I never took my kids skiing. When they were younger and I was developing my career with MSc and PhD studies, and three of them were in private education, skiing holidays were too expensive. Maybe they were just being kind and trying to spare my feelings (because they take after their dad), but the children all said they preferred a summer holiday anyway, when they could enjoy the sunshine and frolic in the water (lovely word, 'frolic').

About twenty years ago, I was asked to give a series of lectures in France, on a course run for English dentists — *at a ski resort!* In return for my (excellent) lectures, they would pay all travel and accommodation expenses, ski passes and lessons, for me and my wife. The downside — they wouldn't be paying me a fee. I told my wife and I think it took us about a nano-second to decide. Of course, we'd go — we had nothing to lose!

For some reason now lost to me, we couldn't travel to France with the main group. So, our hosts arranged for us to go a couple of days later with one other family who were in the same position regarding the timing. Dr Other-Family was a consultant at the dental hospital, and he was travelling with his wife and their young son, George. He later went on to become Dean of the dental school (the chap, that is, not the little boy — although, having said that, George was such a bright little lad, by now he might well be Dean).

***

We met up at silly o'clock in the morning at Manchester airport, to find the consultant in a real two-and-eight, well hammered, plastered, and any other slang terms you can think of to describe the state of being under the influence of booze. Shocking. As we'd never met this man before, we had no clue as to his normal behaviour and were, to say the least, intrigued. His wife, who was clearly as sober as a judge (or as a judge should be when doing judgey-type things) was taking care of little George and seemed not to be at all affected by her hubby's condition.

Hearing the explanation for this odd situation was definitely one of those 'ohhhh, I seeee' moments in life. He was terrified of flying. He told us that, with the help of a certain amount of alcohol, he could just about manage a flight on a passenger jet plane, but he would have to be completely comatose to get on a propeller plane. We all checked in and were soon called to board. Guess what? Yep. Propeller.

With the aid of more alcohol, we managed to get him on the plane. Arriving in France, we agreed that we would hire one large vehicle (I don't mean a fifty-ton artic, just a big car) that would take all five of us with luggage to the ski resort. Just one small point — Dr Other-Family was so far gone by now, Yours Truly had to do all the driving. Notwithstanding, we made it to our destination, parked the (big) car and checked in.

This rather strange start to the holiday (oops! I mean the professional course) actually didn't spoil things for us — quite the opposite, as it turned out, and we enjoyed a wonderful week of skiing, lecturing (only me and Dr Other-Family, not the wives and little George), listening to others lecturing, and socialising. Dr O-F was one of the nicest people we'd ever met — funny, clever, great company, witty — and he was a brilliant lecturer.

All good things have to come to an end, so they say, and when we were packed and ready to leave the resort, we agreed that Dr O-F and I would share the driving back to the airport, and he would hold off having anything to drink, despite knowing the chances were that the plane would be of the propeller variety.

Now, where did I park that car? Even though it was a big car, I couldn't see it anywhere, nor could I remember where I'd left it, and, to make matters worse, it had snowed heavily most of the time we were there, so almost everything outside was buried under heaps of the white stuff. We eventually discovered its whereabouts, and then had to dig it out before we could go anywhere.

The rest of the journey back to Manchester and normality (ish) was uneventful, I'm happy to report.

***

A couple of years after that most enjoyable skiing holiday (sorry, my mistake — it was a week-long dental course in France), I was approached again about lecturing on a 'ski with dentistry' course (how many of these events can there be, I wonder?).

Of course, I accepted. Or rather, *we* accepted. By now, we had become somewhat more efficient regarding the organisation of the days on such a jolly (oops! There I go again — I mean lecture trip), but we did keep things on the sedate side, with a late breakfast, wander over to the slopes, ride the cable car up, ski down then have coffee. Another cable car ride up, another ski down, and that would take us to lunchtime. After a leisurely meal, one more cable car, one more ski down, and into the bar for some *Glühwein*. Then it was Goodnight, Vienna (even though we were in Alpe d'Huez in France).

However, our new companions were of a rather different mind. You had to get up early (and yes, it's still my pet hate), rush your breakfast then ski as if your life depended on it, right up to lunchtime. Everyone got together for lunch, which involved the consumption of a whole lot of alcohol, then it was an afternoon of more non-stop, furious skiing, right up to when the cable cars stopped running. Then in the bar to drink a load more until it was time for — yes, my lecture.

Consequently, I cannot honestly say with any shred of confidence if anyone actually *heard* my lecture, or — more to the point, understood it. But then we'd have dinner, washed down with yet more booze, then we'd re-locate to the bar (rapidly becoming a familiar venue, if a tad blurred) and drink till late.

Eventually, and somehow, everyone dispersed and went to bed. The next morning, the whole fiasco would begin again, way too early. It's tiring, just explaining it.

All I can tell you is that everyone either appreciated my lectures very much, or they couldn't remember a word I'd said (or slurred) — but the end result was that I was invited to return the following year and do it all again.

My wife and I both enjoyed these trips so much that, in the years when I hadn't been invited to speak (how dare they overlook me?), we would pay to go anyway. We've both hung up our skis now — reluctantly, it has to be said — but we keep in touch with some of the regular members, so we still have the contact, if not the manic skiing sessions and alcohol poisoning.

Just a Little Filling...

Here are some little bits and bobs that aren't really grown-up enough to be proper chapters, but they will hopefully make you smile...

I'd been working for Ernie (if you've been paying attention, you'll remember him) in his two practices for about eighteen months, when I made the decision to go it alone and open my own practice.

Back then, all you had to do was find suitable premises, have the relevant equipment installed, and apply for your NHS registration number. Oh, yes, and you needed to be properly qualified.

Your next task was to get some actual real people to come along to your nice new practice and be your actual real patients. The whole process was known as 'squatting'. Because of General Dental Council regulations (file under D for Daft), the dimensions of the plate to be displayed on the front door, proclaiming your name and professional qualifications, were controlled. Even signs to go in windows were restricted in size and how many you could have (even Dafter).

Advertising of your practice was not allowed, and you were supposed to promote yourself, your work and your premises purely by word of mouth — oh, the irony! (you can make up your own joke for that one). Fortunately for the profession, and finally demonstrating some common sense (there is a scary acceleration factor involved in the disappearance of this quality), the Daft GDC regulations were rescinded a few years later.

So, I found suitable premises, quite close to home, above a bakery store in a shopping parade (that's the premises that were above a bakery, not my home). The lady owner of the property — we can call her Miri — became my tough, but fair, landlady. A builder, Derek from Bolton, introduced to me by Ernie, took on the work to transform the premises into a functional dental practice.

At the time, it was common for dentists to get their name plate and window signs up as quickly as possible, so that local people passing by would get to know the new dentist would be open for business in the near future (reliant on two things, of course: one, that the work would be completed in a timely fashion, and two, that passers-by could read). Accordingly, Derek from Bolton organised the door plate and window signs, and these were duly displayed before he started the real work (I didn't suppose that either Derek from Bolton or any of his trade peers would regard fixing a plate on a door and a couple of posters on glass as real work, but I stand to be corrected, as always).

By now, there was a shortage of dentists because people had grown familiar with paying the new NHS charges, and they were keen to have their teeth looked after by an appropriate professional. Derek from Bolton had barely begun work on the place before he was inundated with folk asking when we would be open and could they make an appointment. So, he very kindly started taking names and telephone numbers (that's landline numbers — there were no mobile phones at the time... happy days) and he'd write the details on the bare walls so that I could collect the information next time I was in to check on progress.

My first ever appointments diary — a wall.

***

At the time when I was opening my first practice, an evolution was taking place — the two-car family was born.

Women were starting to drive (formerly a very male-dominated skill, in a time when the womenfolk were not to be encouraged to imagine having their tiny hands on the steering wheel) and have their own cars to go shopping (men getting out of shopping could have been the biggest driving force behind this), to keep medical appointments for themselves and the children, and all of those other things they had previously had to rely on hubby for.

Without wishing to appear sexist (as if I would), I did notice that *parking* a car was not really a strong point with some of our lady patients, and with those other female drivers who visited Miri's Bakery. Once installed in my premises, I'd look down from the window to see various cars all over the place, appearing to be more *dumped* than parked.

Given that this location was on a main road that was also a busy bus route, it was a bit of a miracle that nothing serious befell those poor abandoned cars.

***

When my old friend, Phil, and I were in practice together, we decided that he would take care of all staffing matters (that became 'personnel' which then became 'human resources') and I would look after the finances. I think we agreed wholeheartedly that, if I took charge of staffing and he ran the finances, it wouldn't be long before we had none of either!

***

When we had our practice on Quayside in Manchester, the shopping centre was close by, and we would allow free parking to patients after their treatment so they could go to the shops and not have to worry about getting parked, paying parking charges — and worse, running out of time and getting a ticket.

It always amused me that these people were paying us very large amounts of money (I mean *a lot*) for dental treatment, and yet didn't want to pay the measly sum of £2.50 to park their car in the centre.

This is when some of the husbands of our lady patients started commenting that it wasn't our dental work that was making a hole in their bank account, but the retail therapy afterwards.

***

In one of my earlier practices that I started from scratch, things were going really well, so I decided to expand the practice by adding a second surgery, with the idea of employing a dental hygienist — something not very common at the time, and I felt it would be good for the patients and good for the practice to have this extra (and quite innovative) string to the professional bow. I'm trying not to mention that it would also be good for the bank balance, but I suppose you've worked that out.

In order to reconfigure the practice, I needed the services of an architect to design the layout of the surgery, utilising the existing space. Architect found and commissioned, all went well, then — for some reason that now escapes me (as do many other things) — I went on holiday shortly before the work was due to be completed, leaving it to everyone else in the practice to oversee the finer details. Oh, big, big mistake…

On my return, I couldn't quite believe what had happened, starting with the architect specifying it and then nothing being spotted by any of my fellow professionals. When I walked into my surgery, the chair was fitted at one end of the space and the operating light — that's the light that illuminates the patient's mouth so I can see what I'm doing — was way over there, at the other end. When I questioned the architect as to his reasoning for putting these two vital pieces of equipment *that could only function when together* at opposite ends of the room, he said he thought it *looked better aesthetically.*

Aesthetics, my rear end. I had to have the light unfitted and re-fitted where it should have been fitted in the first place. I vowed never to go away again whenever any work was being done. Lesson learned.

***

Since we all started living in a world where ticking an endless stream of boxes seems to be the chief element in any business, one of those being the much-feared GDPR, we also check patients' dates of birth.

One day, a lady named Crystal came in to the surgery and when we checked her date of birth, we spotted something on her records — her surname. I'm not a betting man but I wonder what were the chances of Crystal marrying a Mr Ball?

And yet, there it was, in black and white — Mrs Crystal Ball!

***

On another occasion, I was treating a female patient who was a rather grand Duchess, a lady slightly younger than myself. Being the cheery fellow I am with patients, I asked her very courteously (I almost felt tempted to bow slightly) what I should call her.

Most people call me Your Grace, came her rather cool reply.

I considered my legs to be well and truly slapped. Not only that, mind you, but when it came to her bill being settled, I had to wait for her 'household' to get around to paying me. Most patients pay on the way out!

***

Speaking of payment, after carrying out some work on a patient who was an extremely wealthy gentleman, I escorted him — as was my wont — from the surgery to Reception. The reason for this apparent professional courtesy, if anyone asked, was to bid the patient a friendly *au revoir,* although the real reason was to make certain everyone paid before leaving the premises.

When asked how he would prefer to pay, the gentleman gazed at me then at the receptionist with an incredibly blank expression, then asked us to call his 'assistant' in from the car park, where she had been waiting in his beaten-up old banger.

Without a word, she took *his* credit card from *her* purse and made the payment. He had absolutely no clue as to how to pay for anything with his own card!

***

I remember this one well…

One of our nurses had gone in to work particularly early to set up a surgery, so it would be ready for when the dentist arrived. For some reason that wasn't clear, she couldn't get any of the electrical equipment to work — the ceiling lights were working but nothing else, and no matter how many times she flicked the switches on the various machines, there was absolutely no response.

Using her initiative (always a worry), she called out the dental engineers — something we would only ever do as a last resort because it was extremely costly — and when the highly technical, highly experienced and highly expensive guy walked in, he took a quick look round, then picked up the three-pin plug extension connected to the equipment… and put it into the wall socket.

Need I say, this nurse's career with us didn't progress much after this.

***

We once had a female patient — let's call her Mrs B — who was extremely nervous when having dental treatment. To make it worse, she had quite complex dental needs. It seems to be the rule that the very difficult patients are the ones who need the most difficult work doing.

Mrs B would repeatedly make an appointment and then either not turn up at all, or she would cancel at a very late stage in the proceedings, when it was too late for us to fill the appointment with another patient.

In those days, the appointment diary was actually a diary — a proper physical book that sat on the reception desk and in which patients' sessions were written. Staff were instructed to write in pencil (as you already know), because many appointments were altered, cancelled, re-scheduled and so on, and pencil was easy to erase and re-write, whereas ink would have to be crossed out and that would make a mess of the pages — especially when you know how many entries were deleted, changed, shifted or otherwise messed about with.

Anyway, I got really fed up with Mrs B constantly cancelling her appointments or just not showing up, and causing us problems (not to mention affecting our income, which I have now mentioned), I told the receptionists that they should pencil in Mrs B next time, then — given that we hadn't heard from her — after a few days, they should rub out the entry and fill the same slot with the next patient who wanted it.

This worked really well for some time. Mrs B's appointments were pencilled in, they were duly erased, another patient took the diary slot, and we didn't see hide nor hair of Mrs B.

Until one day, when the inevitable happened. She turned up, on time for the appointment that was now cancelled — *by us*. If I say she was furious, would you believe that's a gross understatement?

We never saw Mrs B again.

***

With the decision firmly made that I would *not* be acquiring an Aston Martin, my wife and I decided to buy a speedboat instead, as you do. Not a big one, like you'd see moored in St Tropez, alongside the millionaire's yachts that are equipped with every possible luxury, including an Italian waiter to pour your champagne.

We kept our boat in a little marina near our Spanish abode and we had some really wonderful times aboard, even though in the end I reckon it must have cost us more than the Aston would have!

Following a mishap (no, I'm not going to tell you) we both decided we'd train for — and hopefully qualify as — offshore boat captains (I do wonder what an *inshore* captain would need training for). This we did but, for some reason known only to the relevant authorities, my licence came through allowing me to handle powerboats up to and including seventy-five feet (twenty-five metres), whereas my wife, although she qualified just the same as I did, was only able to captain boats up to thirty feet (ten metres). The bizarre part of this was that I had trained on a fifteen-foot boat and she trained on a thirty-footer! As our friends over the Pond say — go figure!

That anomaly didn't bother us, as we weren't planning to borrow the royal yacht any time soon. We carried on having our good times on the water with friends and family, but something quite odd kept happening.

Remember the chap who took me for a spin in his Aston Martin (thereby putting me off the idea for once and for all)? Well, he carried on having problems with his teeth, most of which resulted in more root canal treatments carried out by Yours Truly. After a while, he became something of his own diagnostician when it came to tooth pain, and whenever he thought (knew) he needed my services, he would cut out the middle man and call me on my mobile phone.

Believe this or don't, almost every time he rang me because he had toothache again, I was on the boat. It just happened that way, but he became convinced that we actually lived on the boat permanently, and only came back to the UK so I could work on his root treatments.

As mad as that is, it's food for thought…

***

Some years ago, my cousin and his family rented an apartment for part of the summer, near our place in Spain. Naturally, we took them out on 'the boat'. Their middle son, who was about twelve at the time, was greatly impressed by this, and was fascinated to hear about my other 'hobbies'. He decided that, if all this was what being a dentist got you, then he was going to follow suit.

He really did it! Two years ago, he qualified as a dentist. I'm still waiting for an invitation to go on *his* boat, but hey, who knew I could have such influence?

***

Throughout history, and still today, many famous people have been known to take short 'power naps', or forty winks, as it's called, especially after the midday meal.

I might not be quite as famous (yet) as the likes of Winston Churchill, Margaret Thatcher *et al*, but I can claim to be a member of this elite club, as I do often fall asleep after lunch for about fifteen to twenty minutes, and I do this with great ease. *And* I almost always wake up five minutes before my afternoon start time of two p.m. Okay, I admit, on rare occasions the nurses have had to wake me — but only very rarely.

Most of the time, my napping would take place in the staff room, where I'd be sitting at the table. The nurses would be there, chatting together and not taking the slightest bit of notice of me. Sometimes, as I nodded off into the cosy world of slumber, I would hear them talking about some rather personal matters (not to be revealed here) and had I not been in my almost-asleep state, my eyes would have been opened very wide at hearing these things.

On occasion, I have taken my little siesta in the surgery, lying on the supine (that's laid flat to you) dental chair.

Once, on the day of our practice Christmas party (I mean the party for those in our practice, not that we had a test party first to see how it would go, then have the real party), I decided to postpone my nap until after surgery, before we went out for our jolly.

Suddenly, I was rudely awakened by hysterical screaming — it was our cleaner, who thought she had discovered a dead body!

I may not be a teenager any longer, but *dead* I am not.

***

In some cultures, the wearing of gold jewellery is seen as a sign of wealth and prosperity (obviously) and people deck themselves out with rings, bracelets on wrists and ankles, necklaces, earrings, and piercings in noses and some other body parts not normally visible to Joe Public.

And teeth. Over the years in practice, I have not only been asked, but *told* to construct gold teeth — especially for the front of the mouth — and also to add gold teeth to a set of dentures.

***

On the subject of dentures, during the mid-1970s I had worked in the oldest surviving practice in Bolton, which is one of Lancashire's historic mill towns and also my place of birth.

It soon became clear to me that a large proportion of our local patients in the mature female category had no teeth of their own, not a single toofy-peg among them. They had what we call full-full dentures — that's a full top jaw denture and a full lower jaw denture.

I investigated this oddity and discovered that, in the early part of the twentieth century, it was quite common practice for a father of a female child to pay for all the girl's teeth to be extracted and replaced with dentures when she reached the age of twenty-one and wasn't yet married. This was regarded as a birthday gift (I'd rather have a watch, if that's okay) and also a celebration of her coming of age.

If, on the other hand, the girl was to be married before her twenty-first birthday, the father would do the same, but this would be regarded as part of her bridal dowry (now, there's a piece of history for you to

Google) so that her new husband wouldn't have the responsibility of taking care of his wife's dental health.

Of course, this practice only took place before the inception of the NHS in 1948, at which point dental treatment became almost free. It was also the time when a severe gum disease, known as pyorrhoea, was prevalent in this country, and this was thought to be the cause of some other general physical illnesses.

The other thing I learned from my investigations (otherwise referred to as 'being nosy') was that, in the early days of this bizarre cultural practice, when local anaesthesia was in its infancy, dentists charged extra for administering the anaesthetic, so some of the young ladies had to have their extractions carried out without any numbing of the area (ouch!).

This would save their dear Papa the mammoth sum of 6d (sixpence before decimalisation), which is now two-and-a-half pence in new money.

***

Another dentures story comes to mind…

A gentleman patient came to see me some years ago, and he had existing dentures. On examination, I noticed there was a rather noticeable (which is probably why I noticed it) and strange gap between his upper and lower dentures, in the corner of his mouth on the right-hand side.

I obviously couldn't avoid asking him why this was, and his reply was to take a pipe (of the smoking tobacco kind, nothing to do with plumbing) out of his pocket and then demonstrate to me how the pipe fitted precisely into this gap in the dentures, thus allowing him to puff away to his heart's content, with his dentures firmly clenched together (essential pipe smoking procedure, for those of you who don't know about such things).

When his new dentures were being made, I (obviously) had to repeat this part of the design, because there was no way he was going to give up his pipe. It was something I'd never had to do before, and, as it happens, never again since then.

***

Still on the subject of dentures (I promise I'll change the subject soon), ever since that puking incident when I was a mere dental student, I'd honestly never been comfortable making them for patients (who else would I be making them for?).

During my earlier years in practice, I couldn't really avoid making dentures because, if I hadn't done so, I quite probably wouldn't have been able to make a living.

Anyway, as I became more established in general practice and most people had to pay privately for dentures, I didn't feel comfortable telling patients I didn't make them — I worried that it might make me seem not quite a 'complete' dentist, if you see what I mean.

So, I came up with a way to deal with this quandary (because that's what it was, a quandary). When asked to make a set of dentures, I would (seemingly happily) say *No problem*. Then the patient would ask what the cost would be, and I would quote such a ridiculously high fee that one of two things would then happen: one, the patient would decline (I could always hope), or two, they would accept and I would be able to work with that, because the payment more than made up for my time and effort necessary to produce the dentures in the first place.

Surprise, surprise, nobody accepted for quite some time, then with dental inflation, the high cost didn't seem so bad after all. Drat. So, I had to keep hiking my price up to prevent it appearing reasonable (my goodness, I couldn't risk that).

The result was that people still didn't accept my fees for dentures.

And guess what? I haven't made any since then.

***

A little story (I've never known if it was true or not) went around about a dentist who hadn't got a clue what to charge for dentures. Whenever a patient asked him what the cost would be, he would look them straight in the eye and just come up with a figure that he thought might be reasonable.

If the patient visibly flinched, he left it at that. If they seemed perfectly okay with it, he would add "each".

***

Over the years, I've come to realise I might be a workaholic.

A few years ago, I took a tumble down the stairs at home and landed really badly, breaking my ankle in three nasty places (these places weren't nasty until I landed on them and made them so).

I was duly rushed to hospital, by which time my foot was starting to turn blue, where they immediately repositioned the ankle. Two days later, they operated, which included inserting a metal plate with seven screws, then it was all encased in plaster.

I was allowed home after a further two days — but with the *firm* instruction to keep my leg up for *several weeks*. WEEKS? Well, that wasn't happening, not never.

Because of the nature of the injury (complex, because nothing's ever simple with Yours Truly) and the kind of repair work done, I needed a wheelchair fitted with a special leg-piece so that I could get around. I couldn't find one to hire so I ordered a new one and had to wait a few days for delivery. By coincidence (although some say there's no such thing), I was between cars, having sold my old one and waiting for my new one to arrive. Strangely, I took delivery of both on the same day — not that I could use the car for some time.

After a few days of sheer boredom, I fathomed out that I could get to work in a taxi as long as it had wheelchair access, then whizz around the practice in my new mode of transport, and — best of all — I could work on patients using my good foot to operate the foot controls, while my injured leg could rest on an upturned waste paper bin.

And that is exactly what I did, to save myself going round the bend (although the wheelchair did corner rather well).

***

One thing you learn, after many years in the service, is that you have to weigh up a patient's personality — and you have to do it very quickly.

An example of this is, there are people who like to have everything explained to them in great detail; others don't want to hear anything at all; and then there are those you can't even speak to, so the order of the day with them is — just keep it zipped!

After a while, I found I could gauge which of these three types a patient was, as soon as they walked through the door. There's something in a person's body language that tells you immediately. With some folks, it almost screams.

The other side of this coin, of course (there's always another side, isn't there?), is that many people experience a shift in their personality when they enter a dental surgery: that bolshy, obnoxious chap who just gave the receptionist a hard time suddenly turns into a big gooey teddy bear when faced with The Chair and a neatly arranged assortment of sterile metal instruments. I always found the two hundred and fifty thousand rpm drill had the biggest impact.

This change of personality can be witnessed again at the end of the treatment session — but only with some patients. Some don't hang around long enough for you to see anything.

It's the moment when he or she looks around the surgery with a sort of nervous energy, then leans forward and whispers very quietly, *Could we just have a quick word...* and, glancing accusingly at the poor dental nurse, ... *in private?*

Roughly translated, this means one of two things. Either, if they pay me in pound notes and don't need any paperwork, will I give them a discount? To which the answer is a resounding NO. Or, can they leave their current dentist and register as a patient at my practice, because *it's so much nicer here?* Again, that's a NO, resounding or otherwise.

When patients actually leave the premises, they normally make some comment and the most often-heard ones are

Well, that wasn't half as bad as I expected,
and *Nothing personal, but I hope I don't see you again.*

Don't worry, sir, in your case the feeling is mutual.

***

Remember the story about the teacher we called Haggis?

Well, I knew from old school pals' chat that Haggis lived in Bolton and — like all revenge seekers — I never forgot that fact. Years later, in the early 1970s, a friend and I bought a dental practice in — you got it! — Bolton. Not just any practice, but the oldest in the area. While we were ensconced in said property, it celebrated its one hundredth anniversary.

A thought occurred to me. Because this practice was so well established and long-running, there was a fair chance that Haggis had been a patient at some time — and might even still be! My idea was to call him in for a check-up examination... and get my own back for him confiscating my *bar mitzvah* ring all those years ago!

I scrambled up into the loft of the old building and set to, sifting through every single patient record card, which took a heck of a long time and it wasn't very pleasant up there.

But my resolve was firm (a bit like my neck and shoulders by the time I finished) and I kept going. Have you any idea how many patients pass through such a practice in a hundred years? No? Well, I have now! I searched every card, but found no mention of Haggis (no, I wasn't searching under that name — give me some credit).

Oh, that desperate feeling of my hopes for sweet revenge being dashed on the rocks of a century-old collection of record cards…

Over the years, I've had the ring re-sized a few times (obviously, because I've grown) and I still wear it. It symbolises my shift from boy to man, and it reminds me of a strange experience engineered by a strange character who confused his role as teacher with the ambitions of his spiritual *alter ego*, sad old Vlad the Impaler.

***

Some years ago, the practice I was working in was ready to expand, so the owner was looking for somewhere to build a new, bigger practice.

He found a suitable plot of land and the construction work began, then it carried on, and then, one day, it was finished. Amazing, how these things happen. All the necessary equipment and fittings were installed and finally, the place was ready to be officially opened.

Unfortunately, I was away on holiday at that point, so I didn't get to see the wonderful new place for a few weeks (yes, I admit it was quite a lengthy holiday — anyone got a problem with that?).

As I drove up to the new building, I was certainly impressed (I'm not easily impressed, by the way) by this striking building — a big, beautiful structure, fit for only the best professionals (of course).

But something was wrong. Oh, so very wrong. At the front of this Taj Mahal of dental practices, there was a sign on the door. It read: *Would patients please go round to the Patients' Entrance at the other side of the building.*

So, our patients weren't important enough to use the front entrance?

***

Something I've thought about over the years — not just thought, but seriously cogitated at length — is trying to come up with a really good April Fools' Day joke that I could play on my patients.

Obviously, I'd only be able to do whatever-it-was to certain patients, those who I know appreciate a good laugh, and wouldn't mind being on the receiving end of my whatever-it-was little ruse. Most importantly, it would have to be people who wouldn't take either or both of these things: the joke badly, and their business elsewhere. And, of course, it would have to fit in with what I do, so, basically, dental work. Tricky.

Eventually, I came up with something... what if I could arrange to fit a front crown on a patient on the morning of the first of April (I understand the joke needs to be carried out before twelve noon), and when I finish the fitting, the nurse and I stand back and admire the result, telling the patient how brilliant it looks, and so on — but without letting the patient see a mirror.

The crown — this is the joke bit, so get ready — would be made in a very bright colour, like lime green or electric blue, anything really vivid and eye-catching.

What a hoot!

Naturally, we would have to fit the crown (the joke one, not a normal one) with temporary cement, and have the proper crown ready for when the patient came back (no doubt within seconds, as soon as they spoke to the receptionist!).

I decided this would be an excellent April Fools' Day prank. Sadly, I haven't actually done it... not yet.

***

Back in the early to mid-1980s, I became a rather active member of the local branch of the British Dental Association, and consequently stood for election as a Branch Representative to the National Representative Board.

I was duly elected in 1985 and sat for three (in my opinion, completely wasted) years.

All of the meetings were in London, even though most of the people attending were from out of town, and therefore not only had to travel every time, but, due to the unreasonably early start time of nine a.m., had to stay overnight as that was the only way they could be there when the meeting opened. Nobody wanted to arrive late and have their legs slapped. It was almost as if those in charge were trying to get us *not* to attend!

Despite the number of hotels with rooms in London (I don't know of any hotel without rooms — what would be the point?), it could be difficult to get anywhere decent, especially if some major sporting event was taking place at the same time.

On one occasion, I was having a real problem finding a room and my neighbour, who, by some strange coincidence, was also a delegate, told me he had a spare room booked (a statement that raised an eyebrow and a few questions in my mind, but I could never ask why).

It's a very good hotel, he said, *I always get a really good night's sleep there.*

I thanked him and took him up on the offer (I assume money changed hands at some point, but — just for a change — I can't remember).

I hardly slept at all that night. What with the noises coming from other rooms, doors being opened, closed, locked and unlocked, and the traffic driving constantly along the road outside (I say 'outside' but, based on the level of noise it made, it could easily have been driving through my room), I was awake for most of the night.

When I mentioned this to my neighbour-slash-fellow delegate, and asked him how he had managed to get 'a really good night's sleep' with all that going on, he replied, *Oh, I always take a sleeping tablet — I forgot to tell you!*

***

Once I knew for absolute certain that the Aston Martin was well and truly off the shopping list, never to return, I decided to stick to the decidedly more sedate — but still luxurious, of course (one has one's standards), four-door saloon cars.

My first choice was a Jaguar, the old but great XJ6 model. I ended up owning a few of these, and I enjoyed every minute of driving them, but, eventually, the day dawned when I — or, more to the point, my back — needed something a bit less close to the road surface. Reluctantly, I gave up the Jag and turned to the Mercedes S Class range, four-door saloons with lots of big-boy toys and gadgets, and far more easily accessible for my poor back.

After a while, it became all too clear that the low mileage I was clocking up, just driving to and from work, didn't justify the cost of such a big (swanky) vehicle. And my wife had a medium-sized SUV, so that took care of transporting any goods and chattels or grandchildren that needed moving from one place to another.

I'd always been a fan of the convertible car, and combined with the need to have something smaller, I decided to go the whole hog (no, not the big American motorbike) and look at the two-plus-two convertibles — but they would still have to include as many gadgets as possible.

After testing a few, I settled on (or, should I say, settled *in*) the Volkswagen Beetle Cabriolet. two-litre petrol engine, white paintwork with a grey hood, cream interior, automatic — all-singing, all-dancing. Order signed, deposit paid, and delivery expected in several months' time.

On hearing of my earth-shattering decision, my eldest grandson (who was about twelve or thirteen at the time, therefore under the impression that he was all grown up) asked his father, my son, *Dad, is Grandpa gay?*

Although I had no idea why my offspring's offspring should say this, I did hurriedly cancel my order.

Back to the proverbial drawing board — or, at least, the notepad. This time, carefully avoiding any vehicle with the name of an insect, I decided on the Audi A3 convertible, one-point-seven-litre petrol engine, white paintwork with grey hood, grey interior (I still fancied cream but it wasn't available). Second choice ordered, deposit paid, delivery anticipated in several months' time.

Grandpa's Car by Sammy, aged 11

With some intrepidation, I told the family of this (take two) choice of vehicle. Their gleeful response to my announcement?

Oohh, that's a hairdresser's car!

You know what? I can live with that.

I mentioned that said new car arrived on the same weekend as I took delivery of my (flashy) new wheelchair — no engine capacity to speak of, chrome bodywork, black upholstery, no hood that I could find, definitely manual, all-singing but absolutely *no-*dancing.

I have not only lived with the new car, but have also loved it for the past six years or so.

***

As you know (because you're a bright spark) most doctors and dentists are used to wearing face masks, because it's simply part of their everyday procedure.

Patients, on the other hand, clearly are not. Since the demon Covid era took root, and dental surgeries re-opened, patients have been asked to wear an appropriate face mask (not the Minnie Mouse or Batman kind, please note) when coming into the practice for treatment.

Simple, you'd think — but no, dear reader, you would be sadly mistaken. Some patients just don't seem to comprehend how this works. They sit, or lie back, in the chair and mumble, *Mumm eye name eye math omm?,* which is 'maskspeak' for *Should I take my mask off?*

I really feel like saying, *No, don't bother, I'll just drill through it to get to your teeth.*

But, so far, I've managed to nod and smile, with a polite *Yes, please.*

***

Remember Big Jan? Yes, Jan who wasn't big at all.

We worked together in the 1970s and we began to be aware of something happening that was rather strange — and without any apparent explanation.

Every day, at around three-thirty in the afternoon, the door to the surgery would open — only very slightly, but enough to notice — and then it would close again. The same thing happened every day at the same time, and there was never anyone around who could possibly have been causing it, maybe to play a trick on us (as it was the era of the mullet haircut, flared trousers and platform shoes that could easily cause a broken ankle, you'll understand that we enjoyed a good joke back then). This daily event became a talking point in the practice and we all referred to it as 'the ghost'.

The building we were in was called *Speaker's House* and we thought the name must have come from the piece of land it occupied, which was *Speaker's Corner*. I don't know how true (or otherwise) this is, but in a bygone time in the seventeenth, eighteenth or nineteenth century (I have Googled it but can't find any details, sorry) there was a riot on this site, which sadly resulted in someone losing their life. It was believed (by some — whether I believed it or not is for me to know and you to wonder) that our 'ghost' was the spirit of the dead person visiting the place of their untimely death.

And who knows? Maybe they had been in need of dental treatment at the time…

The R Word — End of A Career

My wife and I are now thinking about moving (or are we now *planning* the move?). I'm not sure which it is, and our present house is now on the market.

This situation, as you know, requires the input of both an estate agent and a solicitor (they call it 'support', but it still comes with a hefty bill).

We were introduced to our new lady solicitor (I mean she's new to us, not that she only just qualified) who told us her father had been a dentist in general practice, but he'd retired at the tender age of fifty-five because — get this — he couldn't stand it any longer, 'it' being dentistry. And what does this man do now? He plays golf.

Two things to note here.

One, I have no desire, intention or plan to do the 'R' thing (I should have warned you, we will refer to the ending of one's career, the cessation of one's working life, as 'R', since I refuse to speak or write the actual word).

Two, the idea of me not working, taking R *and* wandering around a golf course is just wholly idiotic. I enjoy my work, I do not want to stop doing my work, and — as my No. 1 Rule is still (and always will be) SK *(Sport Kills)* — the golf thing doesn't get a look-in.

D'you think maybe I have devised a form of 'reverse retirement' (oh, heck! I used the word) whereby, in my later life, I have turned my work into my hobby, which I enjoy tremendously, which takes up my time and — bonus! — earns me money as well? Answers on a postcard, please.

Recently, my wife and I were chatting about R — not mine, no way, José — but the topic had been raised by a phone call from her cousin in London, whose husband gave up working years ago, and he's still only in his mid-70s. Our conversation went on to why so many professionals among our friends and acquaintances — especially dentists — R early because they can't tolerate the job any longer. I do believe the Covid-19 lockdown situations have contributed to this in a big way, which is understandable.

Because I've reached that age group where people *expect* me to be R'd, they often mention the R word. *Have you retired yet?* (I have to show the word here, because it's a quotation by someone else, although I can't, for the life of me, remember who). I am asked that question all too frequently.

Do they think I'm too old to be working? Am I past it, in their opinion?

Yes, I *am* still fully occupied, I *do* still enjoy my work, and *am* still earning money.

What's the alternative? Moping around the house all day, getting under the wife's feet, and constantly looking for something to do? No, thanks.

I am bemused to see people putting as much time and effort into trying to get *out of* their career as they put into getting *into* it in the first place.

Will I have enough to do all day, every day?

Will I have enough money to do everything I want?

What will I do with all of my time?

Do I need to find some hobbies? And so on.

And when I ask some of the friends and ex-colleagues what they are spending their R time doing, I never seem to get a proper answer.

Well, I get up late, eat a late breakfast, read the paper, then it's about lunchtime. After lunch, I might mooch around Tesco with the wife, or maybe play a round of golf, go home and have an afternoon snooze on the settee, then it's dinnertime. After dinner, watch telly for a while until bedtime.

And the next day — exactly the same.

I don't know about you, but that doesn't do anything to tempt me into the R state. When I ask people, what would I do if I did take R, the reply usually goes something along these lines...

Well... you can relax, take it easy, take your time, de-stress and slow down (like all old folk have to?), maybe learn something new to fill your time.

But I have *already* learned stuff, and I do that stuff now, and I enjoy doing it, and yes, it fills my time —

why, oh why, then, do I need to start doing it more s-l-o-w-l-y? I really don't.

Just a thought (I do have them from time to time) about why some professionals are throwing in the towel a bit earlier than perhaps they had planned…

Dentistry has changed dramatically over the years in many ways — improved techniques, equipment and instruments, more patient-friendly surgeries, awareness and knowledge of oral health and hygiene and so on. But one of these changes in particular, I believe, has led to many dentists, especially in general practice, giving up early. One word. Admin. Or, if you prefer the full word, administration.

The amount of paperwork — now digital, of course, and without a single A4 sheet of eighty gsm in sight, but still requiring the same time and effort — that has to be completed these days is ridiculous. Compiling and typing endless notes (most of which are completely worthless) — GDPR, CQC, GDC… it has almost become a fifty-fifty situation where the admin time equals the actual work time. Yes, really! It seems that our typing skills are almost as important as our dental manual dexterity skills. But we, the dentists, (I'm pretty certain I speak — or write — for most of my professional colleagues) would much rather spend less time with fingers on keyboards and more time with fingers in gobs, if you will excuse the vernacular.

And so, dear reader, when I think about my (one day, sometime, or maybe never) entry into the world of

R, I have decided on the required criteria that must first be met:
- I am no longer able to pour vodka into a shot glass without spilling
- Death (mine, that is)

And please note, I still won't be playing golf.